Getting into

# Physiotherapy Courses

# Getting into guides

Getting into

# Physiotherapy Courses

James Barton

8th edition

*Getting into Physiotherapy Courses*

This eighth edition published in 2016 by Trotman Education, an imprint of Crimson Publishing Ltd, 19–21c Charles Street, Bath BA1 1HX

**Author:** James Barton

© Trotman Education 2008, 2010, 2012, 2014, 2016
© Trotman & Co. Ltd 2002, 2004, 2006

7th–5th edns: James Barton

4th edn: James Burnett

3rd edn: James Burnett & Maya Waterstone

2nd–1st edns: James Burnett & Andrew Long

**British Library Cataloguing in Publication Data**
A catalogue record for this book is available from the British Library

ISBN 978 1 91106 714 6

Typeset by IDSUK (DataConnection) Ltd
Printed and bound in the UK by Ashford Colour Press Ltd, Gosport, Hampshire, UK

# Contents

Contents

# About the author

James Barton has been the Director of Studies and Extra-mural Development at Mander Portman Woodward's London college since September 2007. As well as being the author of *Getting into Veterinary School* and *Getting into Medical School*, James has sat on interview and audition panels and has given careers advice, talks and public seminars across a range of fields, domestically and internationally.

# Acknowledgements

I would like to thank James Burnett for all of his help and input in revising this edition of MPW's *Getting into Physiotherapy Courses*. I would also like to thank Lianne Carter and my family for their supportive words.

I would also like to reiterate the thanks given by the previous author to Alice Holmes, Fiona Pyrgos, Katherine Cran and Tania Dawson. I would especially like to extend my thanks to the Chartered Society of Physiotherapy for the enormous amount of information that they provided during the writing of this book, as well as Libby at Trotman, Lottie and Rachel at UCAS and Katie at HESA. In addition, I would thank Kitty Hudson-Davies and Megan Pudney for their help and creative flair.

The information in this book has come from a variety of sources and is, we believe, correct at the time of going to press. However, the views expressed are our own and any errors are down to us.

I hope that you find this book a valuable and educative tool and wish you all the success in your future endeavours in this field. Remember, life is what you make of it.

Also, an acknowledgement to Caroline. The most innovative physiotherapist I have met.

This book is for Peter Barton and Marjorie Lister.

James Barton
November 2015

# Warming up
## Introduction

Rugby. 2015. A big year for the sport in England. A small matter of a World Cup and the opportunity to watch the greatest team in the history of the sport pick up the ultimate prize. Just as big though, was the introduction of the new concussion laws. Thrown to the forefront of the media's attention, following repeated head injuries to the likes of Welsh international George North, new laws have been introduced to immediately and safely deal with players' rehabilitation back into contact post-knock.

Football. 2015. With eight minutes to go in a crucial match, you have to make a split-second choice. One option leads to potential glory, the other to probable defeat. One means winning at any cost, the other means counting the cost of defeat and dealing with an incensed manager at the side of the pitch. Surely it is an easy decision, is it not? OK, so if you understand the reference, then this is an extreme example of the type of decision that physiotherapists have to make in their careers, but if you are not mindful of the choices that you make, then the decisions you get wrong can often have bigger repercussions. A physiotherapist must be as patient as they are strict and as knowledgeable as they are honest, as rehabilitation is often the hardest part of any injury.

Most people associate physiotherapy with sport and the injuries of high-profile sportsmen and women. For instance, it is not uncommon on a Monday morning, when flicking through the back pages of the paper, to see that Johnny X is being assessed by the physiotherapist after having sustained a knock in the weekend's premiership match. It is a physiotherapist's job to rehabilitate the multi-million-pound stars from their bumps and cuts (and broken bones, torn ligaments, muscle damage, etc.).

At the other end of the scale, physiotherapy can be used to correct smaller injuries, for example those sustained in an accident when the victim needs to learn to walk properly again. It has also gained prominence as a profession because of the leading role it has taken in the armed forces and the rehabilitation work it does with soldiers who have been injured in the line of duty, allowing them to lead normal lives after what are life-altering injuries, and this work needs to be reflected.

In short, physios are invaluable.

Never before has physiotherapy been so much in the media attention; whether from initiatives to get the UK moving and deal with growing health issues, or with physiotherapists having an increased role in the management of a sports team with power of veto and sports stars being suspended for arguing with their decisions. There are also the difficulties the profession faces, with issues ranging from an ageing population to the rise in obesity, to cuts in services. There are many other facets to the profession outside of the treatment room, and admissions tutors require you to be fully aware of that.

I was inspired to write this book after the application of one of my students. He did not get a place to study physiotherapy, despite being a good candidate. He had a good personal statement and a lot of work experience but he focused too much on sport. This book will tell you about the importance of making sure you are not approaching this degree for that reason alone. Universities see straight through that.

Physiotherapy is about so much more than the glamour of sports clubs. Physiotherapy is a competitive degree course. In 2014/15, UCAS statistics reveal that there were 6,230 unique applicants for physiotherapy and just 1,705 accepting places (1,105 women and 600 men), as compared with 6,135 applying in 2013/14. They also show that there were more female than male applicants: 3,485 to 2,745.* Thus, physiotherapy remains a popular degree. Some universities have cut the number of places on offer, though, meaning that there is now greater competition for places. Table 1 shows you approximately how many applicants there are per place. There has been little change in this data over the past few years.

*We acknowledge UCAS' contribution of this information.*

## What is physiotherapy?

The human body is a complex machine that can go wrong for any number of reasons. Physiotherapy is a science-based medical subject that looks in detail at how the body moves; how muscles, bones, joints and ligaments work and how they react to pain and trauma. Physiotherapists diagnose numerous ailments that affect the muscles and nerves, and then proceed to treat the patient, ensuring independence, movement and a return to maximum performance. It is the physiotherapist's job not only to look at the problem and treat it but also to look for any predisposing factors that may have contributed to the patient's ailment and to advise on how to minimise the risk of the same thing happening again.

Qualified physiotherapists work both independently and as part of multidisciplinary teams, ensuring that patients' health and mobility are improved.

| University | Applicants per place (approx.) |
| --- | --- |
| Birmingham | 9 |
| Bradford | 22 |
| Brighton | 30<br>(6 places for overseas students) |
| Bristol UWE | 12 |
| Brunel | 11 |
| Cardiff | 17 |
| Coventry | 15 |
| East Anglia | 14 |
| East London | 10 |
| Glasgow Caledonian | 12 |
| Hertfordshire | 13 |
| Huddersfield | 18 |
| Kingston | 9 |
| Liverpool | 20 |
| King's College London | 16 |
| Manchester | 18 |
| Northumbria | 37 |
| Queen Margaret | 11 |
| Robert Gordon | 13 |
| Salford | 28 |
| Sheffield Hallam | 12 |
| Southampton | 36 |
| Teesside | 33 |
| Ulster | 12 |

**Table 1:** Number of applicants per place at university

## What do physiotherapists do?

Physiotherapists have numerous challenging roles within the health sector. They provide services such as rehabilitation and exercise before and after surgery. Within the wider community they provide services to adults with learning difficulties. They also have a role in the workplace, where they can help to reduce injuries such as repetitive strain injury (RSI).

Chartered physiotherapists work with a wide range of people in many different environments, either individually or as part of a large healthcare team.

Physiotherapists deal with many different situations, including the following:

- patient education. This is very important in physiotherapy and means teaching people the 'correct' way to move and lift in order to prevent or slow the onset of problems such as back pain or RSI (see Chapter 7). This may include helping athletes to avoid injury by discussing techniques and training programmes. Poor warm-up routines, too much training, poor equipment and incorrect technique are common causes of injuries, and all of these can be avoided. Using the idea that prevention is better than cure, physiotherapists are able to show people that very small changes will be hugely beneficial: for example, good footwear, or the use of a wrist support when using a computer.
- helping women before and after pregnancy by advising them about posture and exercise
- helping children to deal with mental and physical disabilities
- developing the potential of people with learning difficulties through exercise, sport and recreation; this could also include the use of specialist equipment
- helping people to deal with stress and anxiety
- helping stroke victims to recover movement in paralysed limbs
- helping orthopaedic patients after spinal operations or joint replacements and treating those debilitated following an accident. Using a variety of techniques to strengthen muscles and improve the mobility of individual joints, activities such as walking can be made much easier for people recovering from hip replacements or those with arthritis or osteoporosis. These methods can also reduce the pain and stiffness resulting from these conditions.
- working with AIDS patients
- caring for those people who suffer from Parkinson's disease (one in 20 people over the age of 40 has Parkinson's disease)
- improving the confidence and self-esteem of those with mental illness through exercise and recreation, while also helping with relaxation and body-awareness techniques

- working with the terminally ill (both inpatients and outpatients) or those in intensive care to maintain movement and prevent respiratory problems
- helping sportspeople recover from injury
- working in large businesses and companies to ensure that employees do not suffer from physical problems associated with their jobs.

Physiotherapists use a range of techniques, including:

- exercise
- hydrotherapy (see Glossary)
- infrared and ultraviolet radiation (see Glossary)
- manipulation
- massage
- ultrasound (see Glossary)
- vibration
- patient education
- movement analysis
- gait re-education (see Glossary)
- heat and cold application.

# About this book

This book is structured very much like a standard physiotherapy session: it requires adequate warm-up, intensive drills and jumping through hoops, before finally seeing the finishing line, only for you to be given a leaflet detailing specific exercises for you to do at home. Stretch and challenge your mind, without breaking your back!

## How to use this book

The competition for places on approved degree courses is intense – there are very few university courses other than physiotherapy that have more applicants per place. Physiotherapy courses receive more applicants per place than do medicine, veterinary science or even courses at Oxford or Cambridge. Typically, a university might receive over 1,000 applications for 40 places. Even if each applicant makes five choices – and not all do – this still works out at around five students chasing every place. As you have seen on page 3, the numbers are often far higher than this. With such intense competition for places you need to think carefully about all the stages of your application: from the preparation that you do before you apply, through to the interview. You should also think about the steps you can take to maximise your chances of gaining a place should something go wrong at the examination stage.

This book is divided into five sections:

1.  an explanation of what physiotherapists do
2.  getting an interview
3.  getting an offer
4.  results day
5.  useful information.

The first section outlines what physiotherapists do and looks at the kind of career you can expect as a physiotherapist. It also describes what the study of physiotherapy involves and the different course structures on offer. Please note that this book is designed to be a route map for potential physiotherapists rather than a comprehensive guide to physiotherapy as a profession. The Chartered Society of Physiotherapy, or physiotherapists you meet during work experience, should be the starting points for more detailed information on what being a physiotherapist entails.

The second section deals with the preparation that you need to undertake in order to make your application as strong as possible. It includes advice on work experience, how to choose a university and the UCAS application itself.

The third section covers interviews and provides tips on what to expect and on how to ensure that you come across as a potential physiotherapist. It also contains a checklist for you to tick off the important steps in making your application.

The fourth section describes the steps that you need to take if you are holding an offer, or if you do not have an offer but want to gain a place through Clearing. In Chapter 9 there is advice and information for 'non-standard' applicants – mature students, graduates and retake students.

The final section provides useful information on fees and funding and details of the universities offering courses, including their entry requirements. Information for students with Scottish Highers, the International Baccalaureate (IB), the BTEC National Diploma or the Irish Leaving Certificate is on page 97. The universities will be happy to provide you with further information on other qualifications.

At the end of the book there is a further information section and a glossary. Here you will find details of sources of further information on physiotherapy and definitions of any terms and abbreviations relevant to your UCAS application for physiotherapy courses.

# 1 | Pressure points
## Careers

It is essential that you are completely au fait with the fundamentals of physiotherapy before you apply for tertiary-level study; that includes knowing about the different career opportunities that the profession presents. The field you are hoping to enter is not a narrow one.

It is equally important, when you have qualified for the profession, that you are quite entrepreneurial in your approach and progressive in terms of your thinking. Physiotherapists are in essence autonomous, as they are able to accept referrals from a range of sources (though professional autonomy is only granted to Chartered Society of Physiotherapy (CSP) members) and therefore you have to consider the business elements of the profession, i.e. balancing treatment with an understanding of how to balance the books. What this means is that physiotherapists make their own clinical judgements and treatment decisions and they also work in reflection, i.e. reviewing themselves and making corrections to their work where necessary.

Physiotherapy is a career that relies on the strength of the individual as well as the ability to work in a team. Physiotherapy as a subject is highly academic and therefore of great value; this means that employment prospects are large and varied. These prospects are not limited to the NHS; there is an enormous breadth of employment prospects that can be found across the different sectors (see pages 10–11).

Physiotherapy is not, however, a profession that involves only physical therapy. Physiotherapists work with people – in most cases people who are disabled, or who have been ill or injured. Physiotherapists need to be able to communicate on a personal level with people of all ages; to be reassuring and comforting; to explain the treatments they are using; and to help patients overcome fear and pain.

Physiotherapists need to be able to assess the needs of their patients and to be aware of the effects of external circumstances such as social or cultural factors.

## Working as a physiotherapist

Physiotherapists work in a range of health and care environments that include hospitals, the local community, private practice, industry and sports settings. The majority are employed by the NHS. Physiotherapy comprises the largest group within the allied healthcare professions with 51,383 state-registered physiotherapists in the UK.

A typical working day depends on whether you are working in the NHS or private practice. In the majority of cases, physiotherapists work in hospitals with normal working days, i.e. 9am–5pm, Monday–Friday. There are occasions when a weekend may be required, but this is symptomatic of the health profession.

The most identifiable example is of a hospital physiotherapist working in the Physiotherapy Department. A calendar booking system is in operation, as in a GP surgery, where they will see many patients per day, each one for an allotted period of time, about a range of problems, such as rehabilitation from broken bones, bad backs and arthritis, for a range of ages.

Those working in hospitals might work on the wards and visit the ward staff to discuss the treatment plans of new patients. Sometimes they then treat them as part of their ongoing care, often taking them to the physiotherapy department. A ward physiotherapist might have half a dozen wards to cover, varying from children's wards, to orthopaedic wards or stroke units. In some cases, a physiotherapist might be required to work in the intensive care unit if it is thought essential to the immediate rehabilitation of a patient.

Physiotherapists in private practice may have more opportunities to travel, depending on the job they are doing. If you work for a professional sporting association, for example, you may find that you have to travel a lot to support the team. Sometimes patients will be referred to you, other times you will need to target your business, and that may require advertising.

The concept of travel is also becoming more common in the NHS as a result of changes, as physiotherapists are doing more home visits to support the elderly.

To qualify as a registered physiotherapist you need to gain an approved degree (see page 19) that has been validated by the CSP and the Health & Care Professions Council (HCPC). If you complete the degree you are then eligible for state registration (State Registered Physiotherapist or SRP) and membership of the Chartered Society of Physiotherapy (MCSP).

As with any career, there are pros and cons to physiotherapy. It is up to you to decide if the pros outweigh the cons. That is why work experience is invaluable, as it will either confirm your decision to pursue the career or demonstrate to you that you should seek an alternative occupation. Physiotherapists have a lot of demands on their time and they often can be stretched to the limit – if you will excuse the pun –

because of the nature of their work, especially within the NHS, where, as a result of staffing cuts, there is more work for an individual physiotherapist. However, the variety and nature of the work is what physiotherapists thrive on and it is a hugely rewarding career, as you get to see the continuing progress of an individual patient over time.

The question of what attributes a physiotherapist needs is a common one. It is easy to say 'be physically fit'; at the end of the day, practise what you teach. Not to be flippant, it is a good point, as in any very demanding job that requires you to be on your feet most of the day, you want to make sure that you are looking after yourself. Additionally, you also need to consider the psychology of the patient. As with the relationship between a client and a personal trainer in a gym, a patient will have more confidence in their instructor if they can see that the instructor takes good care of themselves. Being active is also necessary for clear thinking, as it gives you the energy to get through the week.

However, over and above that, there are other characteristics that define a good physiotherapist. You need to have patience, peace of mind, the strength of character to encourage a patient and firmness to make sure that they achieve their targets. A physiotherapist is a strategist. Each individual one will find their own style – and you should be encouraged to find yours – but it all comes from this foundation and you need to consider now whether you possess those attributes.

## Common career paths for physiotherapists

Once you have completed your BSc in Physiotherapy you will, hopefully, gain membership to the HCPC and CSP, provided that you have taken a course that is accredited by these organisations. To say that there is a standard route is not correct. The main thing you need after graduating is clinical experience, and the usual route will be to gain experience in areas that you didn't cover on your placements, in a rotational band 5 job.

A rotational band 5 job is a general physiotherapist role in which you rotate through the various departments in a hospital, including respiratory, stroke, orthopaedic, etc. Each rotation will last around four months. These are commonly in the NHS or in some private practices and are designed to build up your expertise before you can qualify for the next band (band 6). These bands also equate to your pay scale.

A lot of physiotherapists get their rotational band 5 job through the NHS or by having impressed on their placements during their course. However, you do not have to have worked for the NHS first before going into private practice. Some physiotherapists set up their own practices, but their success is all based on reputation and on building up the relevant experience over many years. As for anything in life, you have to prove yourself first.

Further qualifications are not essential after your degree, but you are expected to maintain your continuing professional development, which is very important and discussed below.

Private practice is one of the more lucrative career moves. Private practice, as an umbrella term, includes:

- treating patients independently for the same ailments as in the NHS
- working for a sports club or a specific team, aiding in the recovery of sportspersons from injury and helping to optimise their performance
- occupational rehabilitation, which means helping people to recover from accidents or illnesses and to return to their normal lives.

There are also additional opportunities to go off on a tangent and get involved in policy development and research, in order to ensure that physiotherapy as a profession continues to progress over time in line with NHS changes and guidelines.

The areas of work available to you as an aspiring physiotherapist are outlined in Table 2.

| Area | Work |
| --- | --- |
| Outpatient clinics | Advising and treating people with spinal and joint problems, or recovering from accidents and sports injuries. |
| Patients in hospital | Treating inpatients, including people in intensive care units – to help very ill people to keep their chests clear of secretions while they are too weak to cough effectively; to keep their limbs mobile while confined to bed. |
| Schools | Working with teachers and parents to support children with developmental movement problems. |
| Workplaces and industry | Advising managers and staff on injury prevention, as well as treating specific problems. |
| Sports and community centres | Promoting health, preventative health education through progressive exercise programmes and back-care classes. |
| Women's health | Advising women on ante- and postnatal care; exercise and posture; managing continence (specialist physiotherapy can also help men with continence problems); following gynaecological operations. |

**Table 2:** Areas of work for physiotherapists

| Area | Work |
| --- | --- |
| Elderly care | Maintaining mobility and independence; rehabilitation after falls; treating arthritis and Parkinson's disease. |
| Stroke patients | Helping people with paralysed limbs to restore normal movement. |
| Orthopaedics | Regaining movement and strength after spinal operations and hip, knee and other joint replacements; treating patients following accidents and fractures. |
| Mental illness | Holding relaxation and body-awareness classes, and improving confidence and self-esteem through exercise. |
| People with learning difficulties | Developing people's potential through sports and recreation; assessing needs for and providing specialist footwear, seating and equipment. |
| Terminally ill | Supporting people with end-of-life conditions, in the community or in hospices. |
| Private sector | Working independently in private practice, clinics, hospitals and GP surgeries, treating a wide range of conditions. |
| Voluntary organisations | Providing expertise and advice in organisations that support people with conditions such as multiple sclerosis and Parkinson's disease. |
| Community | Going in to people's homes and providing a service for those not able to attend clinic. This area of work is developing as a result of changes in the NHS and is more common nowadays. |

**Table 2:** Continued

Table provided by the Chartered Society of Physiotherapists.

# Employment prospects

*'If current trends continue, demand for physiotherapists will outpace supply by 500 each year.'*
*Information taken from the CSP (www.csp.org.uk),*
*with kind permission from the CSP*

The annual statistics for job opportunities for physiotherapists have been on the rise over the past few years and continue to do so, and physiotherapy was removed from the Shortage Occupation List in May 2007. In 2005, a survey by the CSP revealed that of the 2,000 or so physiotherapy graduates who left university in that year, about 53%

did not have jobs to go to after graduation. The Hospital Episode Statistics for 2003–04 revealed the need for more NHS physiotherapists, and the CSP said: 'Over half a million people with injuries were admitted to an NHS hospital in England last year.' However, the picture is no longer as bleak as it seemed then, with most physiotherapy graduates finding relevant employment; and, once you have a job, the promotion prospects are good, with many vacancies at senior level. This growth is continuing on a yearly basis. The CSP workforce review shows that:

- in 2006, 31% of students had found work as a junior physiotherapist
- in 2007, 53% of students had found work as a junior physiotherapist
- in 2008, 60% of students had found work as a junior physiotherapist
- in 2010, 80% of students had found work as a junior physiotherapist.

In the Destination of Leavers of Higher Education Survey by the Higher Education Statistics Agency in 2011/12, 87.5% of physiotherapy graduates had found full- or part-time work.

In 2013, the CSP saw no change in the proportion of newly qualified graduates taking up its full membership package. According to the CSP, the physiotherapy workforce has 'undergone significant growth over recent years', having increased by 41% between 2000 and 2009. The HCPC recorded 51,383 registered physiotherapists as of November 2015. The figure was 48,249 in 2013. In 2010 the Centre for Workforce Intelligence (CfWI) predicted that by 2016, the number of physiotherapists available in the NHS would have risen by 18% from 2010, to 40,536. However, this figure has been deemed too optimistic and revised in view of the latest figures below.

In 2015, the CSP was reporting that the job market is buoyant and there are plenty of jobs out there for the qualified physiotherapist. However, in some areas, reports suggest that there are not enough applicants. The overall picture shows that 84.3% of students in the subject bracket are employed. There are increased career options nowadays with new prescribing powers, though the number of applicants does not reflect the demand. Having said that, according to recently published figures from The Health and Social Care Information Census, an extra 455 physiotherapists were employed by the NHS in England in 2014–15. They reported 23,006 physiotherapists working in England, an increase on the 22,551 from the previous year; a rise of two per cent.

What is important to note is that significantly more physiotherapists are registered with the HCPC than with the NHS. A large proportion (approx. 15,000) of physiotherapists work outside the NHS (for example, in private hospitals, sports clubs or their own private practice), and these are more difficult to track, as the statistics rely on the voluntary membership to the HCPC of physiotherapists. New government policy has increased private sector healthcare provision and so more physiotherapists are now employed outside the NHS. The CSP is concerned that the freezing of senior physiotherapy positions within the NHS will encourage the workforce to look elsewhere for jobs.

In the last CSP workforce review, in terms of the age and gender split of the workforce, the NHS had 84% female to 16% male physiotherapists. The CSP reports that a larger proportion of men train to be physiotherapists – leading to the conclusion that they are more likely to work outside the NHS – and over half of male physiotherapy students are mature students. Also physiotherapists have a relatively young age profile, which means that a surge in retirements is not likely any time soon.

As mentioned above, there is currently an oversupply within physiotherapy, and without being checked it will continue to increase over the next five years. It should be noted that workforce supply in future could also be affected by a reduction in the international and European physiotherapy workforces, as migration of qualified international physiotherapists might increase competition for jobs in this country. At the current rate of increase, the CfWI modelling indicates that there will be an 18% increase in the workforce by 2016, though this is conjecture. The CSP also states, however, that Australia, New Zealand and the USA are recruiting physiotherapists trained in the UK.

The findings of the CfWI suggest that if the number of pre-registration courses in England is maintained at the current level, then the workforce will grow over the short to medium term, but it will plateau within the decade (estimated by 2018–20). If there is a reduction in the number of training places, then there is a risk that there will be insufficient numbers working in the NHS to meet the demand. The courses that are most at risk of being de-commissioned are part-time courses or those that have non-standard entry requirements. Roughly 80% of all qualifying physiotherapy degree courses in the UK are full-time, three-year programmes.

You can maximise your chances of employment by studying for a degree accredited by the CSP and HCPC and also by being a student member of the CSP.

> '*I wanted to be a physiotherapist as I wanted to be involved in sport. However, what I quickly came to realise was that there is no need to be so narrow. The most fulfilling thing about a career in physiotherapy is the variety of cases that you take on that can translate into all fields. I would encourage anyone starting out to think beyond the end goal immediately and focus on the overall learning for such a demanding profession, and in the future, only then, work out what field you want to specialise in. I remember being given that advice by my careers adviser after he drew a red pen through my personal statement that was purely focused on sport. Without that advice, I would not be at university now, as physiotherapy departments do not like such a narrow view.'*
>
> *George, Bristol UWE*

To give you an indication of what pay you could be expecting if you joined the physiotherapy profession, included below is the table showing the NHS physiotherapy pay scales in England from April 2015*.

| Band 2 | Band 3 | Band 5 | Band 6 | Band 7 | Band 8a | Band 8b |
|---|---|---|---|---|---|---|
| £15,100 | £16,633 | £21,692 | £26,041 | £31,072 | £39,632 | £46,164 |
| £15,363 | £17,179 | £22,236 | £27,090 | £32,086 | £40,964 | £47,559 |
| £15,786 | £17,800 | £23,132 | £28,180 | £33,227 | £42,612 | £49,968 |
| £16,210 | £17,972 | £24,063 | £29,043 | £34,876 | £44,261 | £52,752 |
| £16,633 | £18,468 | £25,047 | £30,057 | £35,891 | £46,164 | £55,548 |
| £17,179 | £19,027 | £26,041 | £31,072 | £37,032 | £47,559 | £57,069 |
| £17,800 | £19,461 | £27,090 | £32,086 | £38,300 | | |
| | | £28,180 | £33,227 | £39,632 | | |
| | | | £34,876 | £40,964 | | |

Table 3: Indication of pay scale from April 2015
Content sourced from www.healthcareers.nhs.uk/about/careers-nhs/nhs-pay-and-benefits/agenda-change-pay-rates and http://www.nhsemployers.org/~/media/Employers/Documents/Pay%20and%20reward/Physiotherapy.pdf

As physiotherapists progress in their careers, they are expected to keep up to date with the CPD framework detailed below. As they do this and achieve higher levels of responsibility – and indeed reach team leadership and management roles – they have the opportunity to increase their earnings.

The NHS has a structured tiering of pay grades and you will need to follow their framework in order to move up the scales. However, private practice is of course different and the only regulations really imposed at that point are those assumed by what the market is doing and what other operators are charging within it. In-house private physiotherapy, such as in sports clubs for example, will determine the pay scales themselves. However, pay is always determined by experience and therefore the more emphasis you put on CPD, the quicker you will progress in your career.

## Continuing professional development

Throughout their careers, physiotherapists are expected to develop their skills and to keep up to date with developments within the field in a structured and systematic way. This is known as continuing professional development (CPD). Physiotherapists are responsible for identifying, planning and recording their own CPD, setting themselves targets and collecting evidence in a portfolio to support their CPD. The process of CPD is summarised in Figure 1.

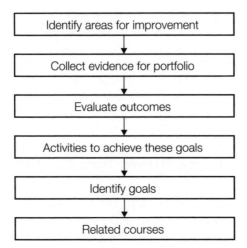

**Figure 1:** Process of continuing professional development (CPD)

## Occupational therapy

While there are a number of differences between physiotherapy and occupational therapy, a lot of similarities are also found. The link is often between dealing with the physical and the mental faculties of a patient in order to ensure their overall rehabilitation. Occupational therapists help people to carry out the tasks and activities that are necessary for them to lead a fulfilling life. These might be work related – helping people with disabilities to cope with their jobs – or they might be everyday things such as cooking, bathing, travelling or socialising. Occupational therapists work in hospitals, for charities and social organisations, in schools and the workplace, in prisons, within the local community and in many other situations. Occupational therapists deal with physical, mental and social needs, for example:

- helping children deal with learning difficulties
- helping people with mental illness to look after themselves, or to be successful in their jobs
- working with accident victims to enable them to re-learn physical tasks
- advising businesses about how to adapt facilities and premises to enable people with disabilities to cope with their jobs
- creating rehabilitation programmes for refugees or the homeless.

To practise as an occupational therapist, it is necessary to follow a degree course in occupational therapy which has been approved by the HCPC and accredited by the College of Occupational Therapists (COT).

For UK students, the tuition fees for the degree course are normally paid by the NHS, with the incentive, and expectation, that you work within the NHS upon graduation. This is not a loan but an award. It is an incentive to work in the profession as opposed to training an individual for private practice, for which the NHS does not receive any benefit. Contact details for the COT and other useful organisations can be found on page 109.

## Case study: Harvey, first-year student at University of East Anglia

Harvey's parents were doctors but his father always wanted him to find his own career path. Harvey had looked into medicine, but decided that it was not the right career for him, based on work experience that he had had. However, a chance placement through a family contact led to him work-shadowing a physiotherapist as part of his school's work experience week.

'That opportunity was revolutionary for me in terms of my future. I had always wanted to do something from a basis of care but medicine and dentistry just did not appeal and I have too many allergies to animals for veterinary science. However, joking aside, I remember one particular patient who inspired me the most. This man had overcome so much adversity after an accident whereby he had broken both of his legs and had been in traction for a year, as well as disturbing his spine to the extent that it was believed he would not walk again. I saw how the physio dealt with him and through his own sheer strength of will, he was slowly turning around that prognosis and forcing himself to learn how to walk again. The role of the physio just cannot be understated in that example.

'So I set about focusing my A levels on my future goal. Though that was not easy, as there are no definite subjects you should choose, apart from a biological science. Therefore, I focused on the subjects I was good at because ultimately you need strong grades. I took ancient history, biology, chemistry and drama and theatre studies, the latter of which should not be scoffed at because it has built my confidence and interaction levels.

'When I was applying for universities, I looked at the entrance requirements of many universities and also rang many of them to get a clear steer on work experience. Following their advice, I spent my A level year and summer holiday taking on a variety of placements to give me a complete picture of the profession and to start building my skills. I firmly believe this is what got me my interviews, as the majority of questions they asked me centred on the work. They quizzed me on what I had learnt and gave me a couple of scenarios to see what my instinctive response would be. I enjoyed the interviews but they were looking to see whether what I had said I had actually completed.

'I learnt so much before I even started my course, from the glamour of certain physiotherapy, to the emotionally resilient work in stroke units. I am very much looking forward to graduating but there is a lot of hard work ahead. My best advice to anyone thinking of physiotherapy is that you can never be too prepared, as the competition is tough. Also, research the universities and their courses. They are all different and will be suited to some but not everyone. Find where you think the course will most benefit you.'

Harvey went to the University of East Anglia after achieving AAA in his A levels.

# 2 | Strengthen your core
## Physiotherapy courses: what to expect

This chapter deals with the types of course that you can expect at university. It looks at the typical structure of a BSc as well as the different teaching approaches you might find. It also discusses courses in Scotland, Wales and Northern Ireland and the differences in course style, as well as MSc (pre-registration) courses. It is useful to note that these are guidelines and that courses can vary between universities, so make sure you research the available courses properly.

In the UK, as mentioned in the previous chapter, a physiotherapist requires a degree from a CSP-/HCPC-accredited course in order to practise with confidence. In turn, if you practise in the UK, you are required by law to be registered with the HCPC. An accredited three-year degree will allow you to register with the HCPC and CSP after graduation. All physiotherapy degree programmes in the UK at mainstream universities are accredited by the CSP. There are 34 qualifying courses available at undergraduate level, 29 being in England, three in Scotland, one in Northern Ireland and one in Wales. There are other, part-time courses, but these are now in danger of being de-commissioned.

Physiotherapy is a very competitive course and, as such, the entry levels will be set higher than the minimum. There are no prescribed A levels that you should take, unlike for medicine, but at least one should be in a biological science. That said, it will always reflect better on you if you have chosen your A levels with your ultimate goal in mind, e.g. psychology would be better as a third subject than film studies. Physical education or sports science is often listed as a requirement, either as an alternative to or in addition to biology. You will need top GCSE grades and competitive A level results, usually in the A–B grade bracket, depending on the academic establishment, with AAA–ABB being a typical offer. However, always bear in mind that entry requirements from universities are the minimum. A lot of people will be applying with higher predicted grades and there is also much more to the application than academic achievement, which we will discuss later in the book.

The key for now is to check each individual universities' website in order to find out the details you require.

# Typical course structure

In accordance with good practice set out by the HCPC, all UK physiotherapy courses are revalidated every five to seven years. While all physiotherapy courses contain many common elements, there are significant differences in the structure of courses, in the course content, in the way in which the practical and patient-contact elements are arranged and in the styles of assessment. You should investigate this thoroughly by reading prospectuses and looking at the physiotherapy departments' websites in order to find out which ones will suit you best.

In line with recent governmental changes, including a move towards the development of physiotherapy in the community and the focus on prevention, many universities have adjusted their course to reflect this and to help students meet the changing state of the NHS and be able to work successfully within it.

A typical course structure will look something like the following.

### First year

Underlying theory and practical issues:

- anatomy
- cardiovascular and respiratory functions
- communication and clinical skills
- kinesiology (the mechanics of body movement)
- musculoskeletal conditions
- physiology
- research methods
- professional development.

### Second year

The second-year course divides time between academic study and clinical placements:

- clinical education, taking into account social, cultural and economic factors
- clinical placements
- neurology
- pathophysiology.

Clinical placements take place in a variety of settings, including hospital wards, physiotherapy outpatient departments and specialised units within hospitals and the community. The clinical placements will focus on areas such as orthopaedics, rehabilitation and community medicine. CSP guidelines require a certain number of hours (1,000) of clinical practice to be undertaken in order to gain recognition, and the 16 weeks of clinical placement usually comprise around 30 hours per week.

### Third year

The third year will also be split between clinical and academic study – students will usually spend about 20 weeks of the course on clinical placements. Specialist areas of study could include:

- burns and plastic surgery
- exercise and sports science
- learning difficulties
- mental health
- neurology
- neurorehabilitation
- outpatients
- paediatrics
- pain management
- respiratory medicine
- ageing studies.

# Research dissertation

There will be continuing modules in research alongside the clinical placements. Evidence-based practice is essential in physiotherapy, therefore students need to learn how to carry out research as well as how to use existing research. For all honours degrees, this is a major component of the course in the second and third years, and there is a focus towards a research dissertation that will be submitted in the final year. This will refine the research skills you have learnt during your three-year course and allow you to demonstrate your knowledge on a relevant topic of your choice.

# Elective clinical placement

At the end of the third year there may be an elective clinical placement. You will choose the specialty in which you wish to work and arrange the placement yourself. Many students choose to work abroad, or in areas of healthcare not previously encountered in their own clinical education.

Be aware of the different teaching styles of the courses and refer to the universities' websites to find all the information. Some courses are modular, some have a lot of emphasis on clinical teaching and others are more theoretical. You need to find out which courses best suit your needs, offer you the opportunities you seek and that will help you flourish.

## Teaching styles

These will be different, depending on the instructor and the course material; however, they can broadly be split into the following types.

- **Interactive:** An interactive style is what the name implies, with discussions, Q&A sessions and presentations. This style suits those who have already absorbed the facts, and students will pursue independent research and build on this through the practical aspects of the course.
- **Lecture:** A lecture is useful for providing a lot of facts in one session, which will then be researched further outside the course. This implies extra reading to supplement what you have been taught.
- **Problem-based learning (PBL):** This is student-centred learning where you will learn about topics by looking at multifaceted and realistic problems. You will work in groups and identify what you know, what you need to know and how you will find the information necessary for solving the problems. The instructor will ask questions and provide resources to lead you to the right answers. However, you must figure the answers out for yourself.
- **Practice-based professional learning (PBPL):** This style requires a level of professional practice in order to fully understand the course. It is in contrast to theory-led learning and is directly related to the practical aspects of the course. It is a new style of learning and is prevalent in the newer universities.

You should look on the websites for the individual universities to find out which teaching styles they use. See Chapter 11 for university contact details.

## Courses in Scotland

There are three universities in Scotland where you can study physiotherapy:

1. Queen Margaret University
2. Glasgow Caledonian University
3. Robert Gordon University.

The courses are four years full time, rather than three years full time as in England. The courses have a strong clinical bias, with work placements, and you are required to complete an honours project in your fourth year.

Robert Gordon University even has a three-dimensional modelling approach (see page 24) to learning as well, which makes the course more interactive.

It is also possible to take a two-year MSc in Physiotherapy pre-registration course or an equivalent MSc in Rehabilitation Science accelerated course after taking a different degree. This allows students another opportunity to study physiotherapy after having studied in a different but scientifically related discipline.

The section below summarises the options on offer on the Scottish courses so that you can see the different approaches of a Scottish university. Apart from the length of course, you will see that they are not wholly dissimilar to the English courses.

## Queen Margaret University

Years one and two are spent learning the basic and applied sciences needed for physiotherapy, as well as developing patient-management and therapeutic skills. Part of your learning will be alongside an experienced, registered physiotherapist, working with patients, carers and/or families. It is important to work with other health and social care professionals to see the role each plays in a patient's care. Practice-based learning is employed in settings around Scotland; this is funded by you.

In the final year, students work in small groups to undertake a relevant project to enhance their skills for work.

The university has implemented an inter-professional education (IPE) focus to allow an autonomous and team-based approach. The aim of this course is to develop a student's understanding of what personal qualities are necessary, but also what the characteristics are of a successful team. This will develop your all-round skills, teamwork, strategy and confidence as well as giving you the opportunity to learn from professionals.

## Glasgow Caledonian University

The aim of this course is to give you the professional and academic knowledge and skills needed to manage individual patients. This course promotes your critical analysis skills, which you will have to use to justify and evaluate evidence in your practical work. This will be particularly relevant in your honours project in the fourth year. Different models of care will be discussed, and you will gain an understanding of the influence of governmental policy on the profession. Healthy lifestyles and physical activity are promoted heavily on this course and placements play a big part in supplementing your learning.

### Robert Gordon University

A very modern course, this is designed to help you 'meet the demands of the rapidly changing health sector'. The clinical placement is of primary importance, as it gives you the 'real' experiences that will ensure your professional credibility.

This is very much a practical course, delivered in state-of-the-art teaching and clinical skills facilities. You will use practical therapy rooms and a human performance laboratory. There is also a 'sophisticated three-dimensional motion analysis system' which will allow you to see in action what it is you are being taught. There is also a unique, computerised 'SimMan' in the clinical skills area where you will be able to practise before going into a real-life setting.

The final year will put most emphasis on evaluation and research skills and two final clinical placements to refine the necessary techniques required for the profession.

## Courses in Wales

The section below summarises the options on offer at Cardiff University.

### Cardiff University

The department is over 100 years old and offers a CSP-accredited degree over three years. The diversity and complexity of the profession are mirrored in the theory and practice elements on this course. It combines university lectures with 'a minimum of 1,000 hours of placement education'. You will learn from both academic and clinic physiotherapists, creating a holistic approach. Students gain experience in all of the core areas of the profession. Placements take place around Wales but may also be arranged in other locations in order to maintain high standards.

## Courses in Northern Ireland

The section below summarises the options on offer at the University of Ulster.

### University of Ulster

In Northern Ireland there is one principal university recognised by the CSP teaching the physiotherapy course, the University of Ulster. One key different feature is its use of peer examination, where a significant part of your learning is assessing the work of others, and this is used as a testing device. As in the other universities discussed above, there is a split between theory and practice, but a large emphasis is placed on practice-based learning. You will have to take the Health Professions Admission Test (HPAT) in order to gain a place at the university. The HPAT is the exam used by the Irish Medical Schools. The test is written and assesses a student's logical, reasoning and problem-solving skills. Non-verbal reasoning is also marked, as is a student's clarity of thought and comprehension of others' thinking.

In each year of the programme, you will usually take six modules, including inter-professional modules. A feature of this course is the integration of theory and practice; participation is expected from everyone and peer examination is used as a testing device. The University of Ulster uses practice-based learning. Beginning in your first year, you will take part in five clinical placements during the course, totalling 30 weeks, to help confirm your learning. Travel and accommodation costs are handled by the student. In the final year, students will undertake either an investigative project or a dissertation.

# MSc (pre-registration) course

This is different from the postgraduate MSc in Physiotherapy, which is for students who have already trained as a physiotherapist and now want to specialise. The MSc (pre-registration) course, for students who have not yet trained in physiotherapy, is a two-year, full-time qualifying programme for graduates with a suitable and relevant first degree. This would usually be a scientific subject based around biology, i.e. biology, behavioural science, physiology, etc. (This course is arguably even more competitive than the BSc entry, because of both the number of applicants and the demands placed on you.)

The course aims to give students with the necessary skills a second opportunity to take on evidence-based physiotherapy programmes with a variety of patients. A large emphasis is placed on the implementation of research and auditing programmes. This course is accredited by the CSP and the HCPC.

### Course overview

The course is divided between research and clinical placements. A large emphasis is placed on the latter, which is typically arranged over six modules with over 1,000 hours of study. Students will treat patients and watch professionals in different settings, from in-house to home visits. There are three core areas: the management of neurological, cardiopulmonary and neuromusculoskeletal dysfunctions, with knowledge from the biomedical and psycho-social sciences recruited as required.

### First year

The first year develops practice and reasoning in the core areas of practice. Evaluation and critical analysis are key to development in terms of physiotherapeutic concepts. In the last part of the year students begin their research project.

### Second year

The clinical modules and research project continue during the second year. There will also be work on an Advancing Physiotherapy module, which addresses other approaches to the management of physiotherapy.

# 3| Pulled in every direction
## Work experience

According to the CSP:

*'Gaining work experience is helpful but can be difficult to organise in physiotherapy because of current training pressures on relevant departments. However, work experience in any aspect of health-care will be useful to you. This is because admissions tutors are looking for evidence that you can communicate well with all ages and sections of the community. Have a look into work experience and try: your local hospital and their physiotherapy department(s) (private or public); private physiotherapy clinics; sports clinics, football clubs, special schools and units (for disabled children and adults), and nursing homes; voluntary work (eg Red Cross Association, St Johns Ambulance Society, MS Society).'*

*Information taken from the CSP (www.csp.org.uk), with kind permission from the CSP*

Equally, the current guidance on the Physiotherapy BSc page of the University of Nottingham's website (www.nottingham.ac.uk) is:

*'Physiotherapy is a vocational degree and applicants need to be enthusiastic about the profession and sure in their own minds that they really want to be a physiotherapist. We require you to under-take as much physiotherapy work experience as possible primarily within the NHS hospital and community settings before applying. Experience in other areas, such as special schools, private practice, sports clinics, and centres for the elderly will strengthen your appli-cation. It is important to note that without work experience it is likely that your application will be rejected.'*

*Nottingham University*

As has been mentioned at many points in the previous chapters, work experience is vital if you are to be considered for a place. It is your guide to the profession at first hand. Without evidence that you have worked with people in the community, preferably within the NHS, you will not be offered a place. Although not all universities are as explicit as Nottingham, most will emphasise the need for work experience. For example, Brunel University's website (www.brunel.ac.uk) says that all applicants are advised to undertake 'an observational clinical experience' with a chartered physiotherapist and St George's says: 'Work or voluntary experience in a medical or health-related field; and an ability to demonstrate a broad awareness of the scope of physiotherapy.'

Although work-shadowing physiotherapists in specialist areas such as sports clinics or private practices is useful experience it is generally not enough, and applicants without some contact with NHS hospitals are likely to find it hard to get an interview or an offer. If you are very lucky (and very determined) you may be able to get a paid job in an NHS hospital as a physiotherapy assistant. However, because of school or college commitments, this is usually only possible during a gap year. It is more likely that you will have to settle for an unpaid volunteer position either on a part-time basis (at weekends or in the evenings) or for a short period of time in the school holidays.

However, current training pressures on hospital-based physiotherapy departments will make it more difficult to get any relevant work experience, so anything within a health-related or care field will also be very useful.

If you are unable to arrange either of these you should try to shadow a physiotherapist for a day or two, and supplement this with a volunteer job in another caring environment such as an old people's home, a hospice or the children's ward of your local hospital. There is also 'A Taste of Medicine', set up by St George's Medical school, www. tasteofmedicine.com, which gives students an insight into the profession and also signposts opportunities for suitable experience.

There are also projects overseas, about which you can find out more at www.projects-abroad.co.uk/volunteer-projects/medicine-and-health care/physiotherapy, which can be just as useful as UK-based work.

Be fastidious in your investigation of how much work experience is required per institution. The universities' own websites are your starting place, followed by contacting the university if it does not publish the information.

## Length of time

While there are no rules about the minimum length of time that you should spend doing work experience, volunteer work or work-shadowing, as a general rule those candidates who can demonstrate commitment by doing something on a regular basis throughout the year or who have spent at least two weeks in a hospital environment are likely to be in the strongest position. In the current economic climate this will be difficult. Think outside the box and volunteer in hospices, schools or old people's homes and watch the nurses and physiotherapists there. You can also chat to physiotherapists or go to physiotherapy appointments with friends or relatives.

*'Get as much experience as you can – it doesn't just have to be as a physiotherapy assistant. Be determined: there is always a way to get in if you really want to.'*

Katherine, University of Hertfordshire

Hospitals will often provide an opportunity for students to do a one-day work experience, and you should contact them directly regarding these opportunities.

Some schools operate schemes where they arrange work experience for you. This saves you the hard work of contacting hospitals or clinics, but the disadvantage is that you will be unable to impress the selectors with your dynamism and determination because you will not be able to say 'I arranged my work experience myself'.

If your school does not operate such a scheme you have two options: to use any contacts that your family or friends have, or to approach local hospitals. To do the latter you need to get the names and addresses of local hospitals with physiotherapy departments and physiotherapy clinics from the internet. You should send an email to the hospital or clinic and include the name of a referee – someone who can vouch for your interest in physiotherapy as well as for your reliability. Your careers teacher, housemaster or housemistress or form teacher would be ideal. An example of a suitable email is given below.

From: Jo Carter
To: volunteers@grantchesterhospital.org
Subject: Volunteer work

Dear Sir/Madam

I am in the first year of my A level studies and I am interested in a career in physiotherapy. In order to find out more about physiotherapy I would like to work as a volunteer in the physiotherapy department. My interest in physiotherapy has grown from studying hip flexors and hip replacements in a Year 9 Biology taster class, and I have been fascinated by the human body ever since. I would be interested in any times you had available, and I will then be able to discuss it with my school, who are very supportive of my application. I would be extremely grateful if I could arrange a time to meet you and hopefully impress on you in person the type of student I am and my resolve to follow this career.

If you require a reference, please contact my careers teacher:
Mr S Boils
Head of Careers
Grantchester Academy
Grantchester
GR8 2BD

I look forward to hearing from you.

Yours sincerely,
Jo Carter

As well as helping you to decide whether you are serious about physiotherapy and adding weight to your application, work experience is useful because you may be able to get one of the people you work with to give you a reference, which you could send in support of your UCAS application or produce at your interview.

## Work experience in Wales

It is very difficult, if not impossible, to get work experience in NHS Wales if you are under 18. Cardiff University therefore does not stipulate work experience as being essential but does want to see that applicants have spoken to physiotherapists or physiotherapy students, that they have looked at physiotherapy-related publications and they have contacted the CSP (which has a pretty comprehensive careers page).

## Things to look out for during work experience

### The variety of treatments available to patients

Make sure that you know what you are observing. Ask the physiotherapist or nurse for the technical names of the procedures that you see, and for information on the techniques and equipment used. Ask about the advantages and disadvantages of different types of treatments, and in what situations they are used. Keep a diary of what you saw on a day-to-day basis so that you can use it to revise from prior to an interview. There are a number of websites that provide detailed information on medical conditions and treatments, and you could add further detail to your diary using one of these. See the list of 'Useful websites' at the end of the book (page 111).

### Working as a physiotherapist

Ask the physiotherapist about his or her work life. Find out about the hours, the pay, the demands of the job and the career options open to physiotherapists. Find out what the physiotherapists like about the job, and what they dislike.

**Case study: Kitty, third-year student at University of Nottingham**

'I come from a long family of teachers, and I assumed that this would also become my career path too. However, a rowing injury in my GCSE year not only was incredibly painful, but in turn altered the course I was heading for. It was fascinating watching the meticulous attention to detail of the physio who looked at my shoulder and through many more appointments I learnt more about the physio's role, now realising that this was something I wanted to investigate further. I know there is more to physiotherapy than sport – I wouldn't be doing it if it was that limited – and that you should never discuss sport as your reason for studying the career; however, everything has a creation point and this was mine, stemming from a personal injury and a respect and appreciation for everything that the physio was able to do for me.

'Looking into it in more detail, I chose my A levels based on the university requirement for physiotherapy; biology and PE, combined with history and English literature. Strange combination as that was, I do believe it was the diversity of the mix and all the different skills I learnt doing it, which made the difference for me. From there, I achieved my A level grades of AAB and went to university.

'I remember the application period itself. It is tricky if you do not know what you are doing; it can resemble a minefield I suppose. However, I was fortunate enough to have a good adviser. If I had two bits of advice for you, it would be to make sure you get help and don't belligerently go about the application believing you know best; and also, visit the universities. The courses are quite different at times from place to place so you will only find out which work for you by talking with the staff and students there and finding out more. Yes, information is on the websites, and you should read them, but there is little substitute for talking face to face and getting a sense of whether the environment and teaching style is right for you. Remember, the feel of the place is important too.

'With apprehension I started at the University of Nottingham, moving into my halls on the first day with trepidation. After the (unforgettable) memory of fresher's week I began to become familiar with the independence of university life. Whereas at school there was a constant monitoring system, registrations and scheduled teacher meetings, university was a more self-motivated experience, though in a degree such as physiotherapy, you do have mentors and are monitored heavily. If I didn't attend lectures or seminars it was viewed as my own problem as I would fall behind, but we were also warned that we would very quickly be asked to leave the course as this is training for a career and you are learning to be a professional. Independent investigation into my subject using the endless university tools and resources was key to my first-year experience. Socially, the experience was fantastic too; the hall system at Nottingham meant that friends were literally right on your doorstep. The SU-organised events such as hall dinners and nights out were a great way to meet people quickly.

'Second and third year moved to a much more seminar-led timetable. These seminars encouraged discussion between my peers and myself to be able to fully explore the ideas within each module. I became comfortable with presenting my opinion to a large group of people and developed key communication skills.

'Then there were the clinical placements. I loved and hated these. It is fantastic to be able to put into practice what you have been learning on the course, and few degrees allow such on the job experiences. That said, they are daunting, you are in at the deep end and often you are faced with a difficult situation. You also cannot always choose where you are placed and the expectation on you is high to get it right from patients and staff. I have had to quickly learn to adapt to survive and now that I have learnt that, I fear no challenge.

'The skills I had learnt in my first two years were vital to my third year; using my independent study skills to research the archives of the library and online resources. I made one error, in choosing a topic far too broad and ended up with a huge amount of information but no clear direction or structure. My tutor really helped me with this and I now feel much more secure of my topic. My advice to you is to use the tutors as they are there to help. However, unlike school, make sure you are proactive enough to ask for the help as they will not find you. This is an adult world and you can quickly find yourself going down the wrong route without proper guidance. This is a wonderful career and I cannot wait to get started.'

## Tips for work experience

- Dress as the physiotherapists dress: be clean, tidy and reasonably formal. There are no strict rules here. You should dress professionally – some wear a shirt and tie, in sports physiotherapy you might wear shorts and a polo shirt, and hospitals have their own specific uniforms. Use your common sense!
- Offer to help the physiotherapist or the nurses with routine tasks.
- Show an interest in everything that is going on around you.

*'My mother worked as an occupational therapist and so I was able to gain extended experience in four major hospitals in the London area. This was absolutely invaluable in showing me that I wanted to study physiotherapy. This experience was divided between working in mental health and working in the community in order to get a real feeling for getting information across and working as part of a team.'*

*Trevor, Bristol UWE*

## Discussing your work experience at interview

If you are fortunate enough to be called for interview then you can expect to discuss your work experience. It is a great way of an interviewer getting to know you and finding out more about your research.

So, remember these golden points about the purpose of work experience to mention in the interview:

- confirmed your choice of study
- important for learning skills, which include: teamwork, independence, administration, etc.
- working hours
- care-based profession.

All the time with work experience, keep remembering what you are learning from the experience. The weakest applications are the ones that just mention work experience for the sake of it. There is nothing worse than a personal statement or interview with just a catalogue of work experiences but no substance behind them, as that is pure vanity. Work experience will form the basis of your discussions. Make some notes about what you learn as you go and take those notes with you on the day of your interview.

# 4 | On the rack/under observation
## The UCAS application

In order to gain a place at university you have to submit a UCAS application. Before you do this, however, you need to be sure that you have investigated physiotherapy as thoroughly as you can. You need to do this for two reasons.

1. You must be sure that physiotherapy is the right career for you.
2. You must demonstrate to the university admissions tutors that you are aware of the demands of the profession.

With so many applicants for every university place, the selectors need to be sure that they do not 'waste' a place on someone who will then drop out of the course or the profession. The number of applicants per place (approximate) varies, depending on the institution; for example, Birmingham has nine applicants for every place, whereas Northumbria, at the opposite end of the scale, has 37 applicants for every place (see Table 1 on page 3). For this reason your application has to be very convincing. Most people's exposure to physiotherapy is limited, and so you need to investigate the profession in depth.

## Choice of university

Once you have completed your work experience and are sure that you want to be a physiotherapist, you need to research your choice of university. There are various factors that you should take into account:

- the type of course
- the entrance requirements (see page 40)
- location
- whether you will be taught alongside students on other healthcare courses such as radiology, nursing, occupational therapy or podiatry.

### Research

The first thing to do is to get hold of the prospectuses. If your school does not have spare copies, telephone the universities; they will send you a prospectus free of charge. You can also order these online, which is the quickest way of doing these, and most have a downloadable PDF for you to look at too. All universities have very informative websites that carry extra information on admissions policies. Once you have narrowed down the number of universities to, say, seven or eight, you should try to visit them in order to get a better idea of what studying there would be like. Your school careers department will have details of open days (or you could telephone the universities directly). Equally, you can look on the website and, for those that have the facility, use their online booking system for open days. Open days always get fully booked, so the earlier you do it, the better. Some universities will arrange for you to be shown around at other times of the year as well.

> **TIP!**
>
> Do not simply select your universities because someone tells you that they have good reputations or that they are easier to get into, because you will be spending the next three or four years of your life at one of them, and if you do not like the place you are unlikely to last the course.

Apart from talking to current or former physiotherapy students or careers advisers, there are a number of other sources of information. The *Guardian* newspaper publishes its own league table of universities, ranked by a total score that combines the university's teaching assessment, a 'value added' score based on the class of degree obtained compared with A level (or equivalent) grades, spending on facilities and materials, student/staff ratios, job prospects and entrance requirements. *The Times* also compiles its own table. The *Guardian*'s tables can be found at www.theguardian.com/education/universityguide.

Of course, league tables tell you only a small part of the whole story, and anyone who makes their choices solely on this basis without visiting the universities or reading the prospectuses is taking a serious risk.

## Open days

Making your choice of university should not be approached without going to the open days of those universities where you are thinking about applying. Going to open days also gives you the opportunity to ask an admissions tutor any questions that you might have about the university generally, such as about sporting activities, societies or accommodation. You should go with a list of questions and show yourself to be proactive. After all, you would not go shopping for clothes without trying them on! Details can be found on the university websites.

Try to go to as many open days as you can, providing you are allowed to by your school. If you cannot attend the open day, go and have a look on another day and email any questions you have to the admissions tutor. Do not ask questions to which you can find answers for yourself on the website, such as 'What is the grade requirement?'; this does not show you to be proactive, just lazy. Ask for details, not generics.

# Academic requirements

## A level reform

In his previous post as Education Secretary, Michael Gove announced his intention to make significant changes to the A level system. These educational reforms came into effect in September 2015. The aim behind the new reforms is to move towards a linear model, thereby creating students who are better equipped for university as a result of a rigorous final examination as the culmination of two years' study. Students will be able to sit examinations at the end of the first year but they will not count for the final result, unless they are dropping that subject at the end of the first year, in which case they will get an AS grade. The new reforms are being implemented in three phases.

**Phase One:** Biology, Business Studies, Chemistry, Economics, English Literature, Physics, Psychology and Sociology.

**Phase Two:** Dance, Drama and Theatre, Geography, Music, Modern Foreign Languages (French, German, Spanish), Physical Education and Religious Studies. These subjects are available for first teaching in September 2016.

**Phase Three:** Accounting, Archaeology, Classical Civilisation, Design and Technology – Product Design, Design and Technology – Fashion Design and Development, Environmental Science, Further Maths, Government and Politics, History of Art, Information and Communications Technology, Law, Mathematics, Media Studies, Philosophy and Statistics. These subjects are for first teaching in September 2017.

Overleaf, you will find a chart (Figure 2) that clarifies what will be available for examination in which year over the course of the next four years, though the summary is:

2016 – All AS and A2 modules available for re-take.

2017 – All AS and A2 modules available for re-take and last opportunity in Phase One subjects.

2018 – AS and A2 modules available for re-sit in Phase Two (with last opportunity) and Phase Three subjects.

2019 – AS and A2 modules available in Phase Three subjects only.

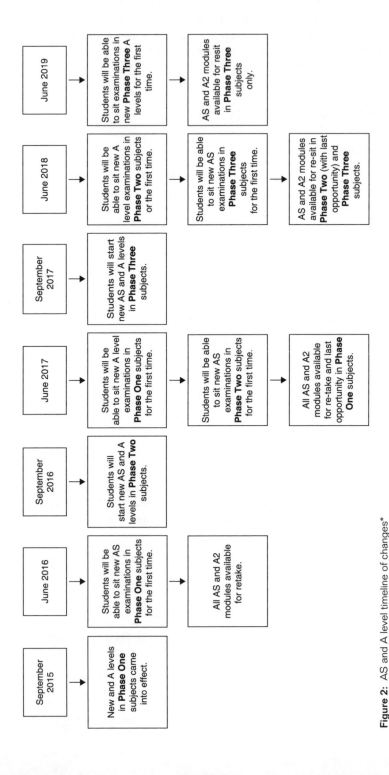

**Figure 2:** AS and A level timeline of changes*

*Based on information taken from: www.gov.uk/government/publications/timeline-of-changes-to-gcses-as-and-a-levels/changes-to-gcses-as-and-a-levels-that-will-affect-each-current-school-year-group.*

*\*This timeline is correct as of December 2015, but please make sure to check the government website for the latest up-to-date information.*

What impact does this have on you? Well it depends on the positioning of the school. Is the case that they are going for a 4:3 AS/A2 split on subjects or a 3:3 split, now that universities have said that they mostly will not be using AS in the offer grades any more? If they decide to do 4:3 AS/A2 split, then the school has a choice whether to enter students for exams at the end of the first year. If they do this, they run the risk of raising your profile before you are ready, as universities may regard your results as an indicator of your progress. That said, the national examinations, though they will not count for the final examination results, would be good practice. Therefore, in both eventualities, even though this is a two year qualification, you must make sure you treat the first year exams as formal qualifications.

The picture is still a little unclear at the moment and many schools will be watching to see what others do before making the decision themselves. What other implications does it have for you? Well, what it means is that GCSE grades are more important than ever before and, obvious as it sounds, you need to manage the transition from GCSE to the first year of sixth form more effectively than in recent years, as there is no room for slow starts.

The outgoing system is still in operation, though it is now being phased out.

In addition to the grades required at A level and AS, all of the universities specify the minimum grades that they require at GCSE. This varies from university to university, but it is unlikely that you will be considered unless you have at least five or six GCSEs, including science, English and mathematics, taken at one sitting and at grade A/B or above (check specific university websites for the exact requirements). If your grades fall below these requirements you need to get your referee to comment on them, to explain either why you underperformed (illness, family disruption, etc.) or why they expect your A level performance to be better than your GCSE grades indicate.

## AS

The term still exists, though under the reforms it is only worth 40% of the final total grade. Students following the A level system should also work hard to ensure that they gain good grades at AS. Remember that how well you do is important from the start. Even though most universities no longer have an explicit AS grade requirement, they are a useful indicator as to how the overall A level will go. Equally, if you sit a public examination in it, or choose to drop a subject and take the AS in it, those marks, while they will not count in a full A level qualification, may consciously or unconsciously be used by universities as an indicator of your likely A level grades.

Imagine the situation: the selector has one more interview slot to fill, and has a choice between two students with identical work experience, GCSE results and A level predictions; however, one has scored DDDD at AS, and the other achieved AAAA. Who do you think will get the interview?

However, an understanding of a subject does not mean that you will gain a high grade at AS or A level, as the examiners have very specific requirements. Mark schemes can be found on the examination boards' websites (see page 111 for details).

# Entrance requirements

Entrance requirements vary from university to university, but a 'standard' offer might ask for a minimum of 128 points (under the new Tariff; or 320 for 2016 entry) from three A levels, including three 4-/6-unit awards or equivalent. The offer will probably specify that biology must be studied to A2 level, along with one other science. A* grades are not usually asked for but do represent higher points. It is most common that you will be given an offer based on getting three grades, as opposed to points. It is worthwhile checking your offer conditions when they come through, to see whether points are also accepted.

An offer of 128 points (under the new Tariff; or 320 for 2016 entry) would be satisfied by a student who gained BBB at A2 level (6-unit awards) and an E at AS (3-unit award). However, this is not the case for all universities.

You should also check the university prospectuses for details of A2 level and AS requirements. Some universities, for example, specify that they require one of the AS subjects to be an arts subject or humanity, rather than them all being science subjects or mathematics.

## The new UCAS Tariff

*Please note that these will come into effect in university offers for courses starting in September 2017 (for applications from September 2016).*

With the introduction of the new A level reforms, UCAS has also produced a new Tariff for applicants that is considered to be more accurate in light of the fact that an AS is now worth only 40% of the overall total. Essentially, qualifications are to be given a size band of 1 to 4, which will be determined by their guided learning hours. They will then be given a grade band of 3 to 14. Those two scores are multiplied together and that gives the overall total.

The part that affects students is shown in the table below:

| Qualification and Grade (Applications starting from September 2016) | Tariff for entry until September 2016 | Tariff from September 2017 entry onwards |
|---|---|---|
| A level grade A* | 140 | 56 |
| A level grade A | 120 | 48 |
| A level grade B | 100 | 40 |
| A level grade C | 80 | 32 |
| A level grade D | 60 | 24 |
| A level grade E | 40 | 16 |

**Table 4:** UCAS Tariff conversion chart

However, what UCAS does say is that a lot of universities do not use the Tariff system and rely solely on grade offers; so do not worry unnecessarily about this new Tariff, instead focus on getting those grades.*

*We acknowledge UCAS' contribution of this information.*

## Your choices

There are five spaces in the UCAS application, all of which may be used for physiotherapy courses. (In contrast, students applying for medicine, dentistry or veterinary science may use only four of their five choices for such courses.) You do not have to fill all five spaces with physiotherapy courses. The key to note here is that universities cannot see who else you have applied to and the order on the form is alphabetical, so you do not have to know your order from the outset. Only once you have got your offers will you put down Conditional Firm and Conditional Insurance. Therefore, you are allowed to apply for a mixture of physiotherapy courses and non-physiotherapy courses, or to leave spaces blank. Thus the important part is the personal statement as it must be written to reflect the course you are applying for at university. As all the courses have to be reflected in the same personal statement, they all have to be broadly similar in order to be sure that the personal statement can be tailored to each of your five choices without any ambiguity in terms of what you are applying for.

If you are worried that you might not be offered a place to study physiotherapy and you would consider other courses, you might want to put down four physiotherapy courses and one other course. The one non-physiotherapy course should be related to physiotherapy, either directly (occupational therapy, podiatry) or in a related discipline such as human biology, physiology. Other courses, such as radiology or nursing, are not related for example. You should not enter fewer than four physiotherapy courses in the application – if you do you are unlikely to convince the selectors that you are genuinely committed, not because they will know where else you have applied, but because your personal statement will not reflect physiotherapy as much as it should.

### TIP!

Whatever you do, avoid putting down medicine or veterinary science as your other choice, because it will be obvious to the selectors that you are not committed to physiotherapy. Equally, if you want to apply for medicine, including a physiotherapy course on your form will be seen as a lack of commitment to medicine.

If you decide that you would be happy to accept an alternative if your application for physiotherapy is unsuccessful, by all means choose another course, as long as you feel able to justify the choice at interview. However, our advice is to apply only to physiotherapy courses because:

- the way you write the personal statement should demonstrate to the selectors that you are committed to becoming a physiotherapist
- you do not run the risk of feeling obliged to accept a place on a course that, at heart, you do not wish to take. If you are unsuccessful in your initial application for physiotherapy you may be able to gain a place through Clearing, if you have accepted no alternative offers.
- the more places you apply to, the more chances you are giving yourself.

Once you have made your final choices, make sure that you have entered the details into the application correctly. More advice on this can be found in *How to Complete Your UCAS Application* (Trotman Education).

*'In order to work out which university to go for, you need to visit each one. That is how I chose Northumbria. I just got a sense from the place when I visited for an open day. Everyone was so helpful and the way they presented the course made it sound like such a dynamic approach. I was impressed with the facilities and the quality of the teaching staff. Moreover, I was encouraged by the options for placements during the course and heartened by the employment rates upon graduating. It is personal to everyone, but you must base that decision upon three factors: overall feel of the place, whether the course has the approach that benefits your individual learning style and the graduation rates.'*

*Kate, Northumbria*

# The UCAS application form

The UCAS website has changed, but only in the sense that it is more user friendly. The UCAS application remains the same and is made up of several important sections. The form is straightforward but it does take time to fill in so do not rush it, as that is when you make mistakes. The sections are as follows:

- Personal Information: basic information – address, telephone number, nationality, fees category, criminal convictions, special circumstances and mandatory information
- Additional Information: equal opportunities, parental occupation and additional qualifications
- Choices: your five researched university choices
- Education: every school you have attended and the academic qualifications you have received while there – GCSEs (IGCSEs), Advanced Subsidiary (AS) and Advanced (A2) level. You must put down every subject that you have been certificated for. If you have not yet received a grade, you put pending in the grades box. Enter only the AS grade of the subject you are dropping and enter the other subjects as A2 grades and categorise as pending.
- Employment: this is only for paid work, not for any work experience – you should write in the employer's name and address.
- Personal Statement: a 4,000-character (including spaces) statement detailing why a university should choose to accept you. Importantly, it should include details of your work experience as the main section. Remember, this is not an essay. Do not use anyone else's words for your personal statement – remember that UCAS has software that will detect this. Check what you have written for accuracy of spelling, punctuation and grammar. Do not be too emphatic. Let the content be what will impress an admissions tutor, not your ability to use synonyms (see Chapter 5).
- Review: check your application before you complete it.
- Reference: this is very important. If you are applying through a school, your tutor will write a statement supporting your application and endorsing your potential for the course. Every school has its own guidelines, but in general the reference should comment on your skills, your abilities and your academic results to date, provide the reasons for any poor results and an explanation of what is being done to rectify this, and also a recommendation to the university of you as a student. If you are applying as an independent candidate, you will need to find an academic or professional referee who will follow these guidelines and seek references from other sources to bolster their reference. Referees should read the 'Advisers' section on the website.

Do not rush the application. Take your time and pay attention to the details. Make sure that you have used the correct course and institution codes. Check that you have entered the correct examination boards for your subjects and that all of the dates are accurate. Ensure accuracy throughout the form. Do not miss the deadline.

For physiotherapy, the following should also be your guide.

Application checklist

- At least two weeks of NHS work-shadowing?
- Voluntary work?
- Right GCSE subjects and grades?
- Right A level subjects?
- On target for required grades?
- Looked at all the universities' prospectuses?
- Open days?
- Minimum of four physiotherapy choices in the UCAS application?
- Personal statement demonstrates commitment, research, personal qualities, communication skills and manual dexterity?

For more details about UCAS and filling in your application, see *How to Complete Your UCAS Application* (Trotman Education).

## Making your application stand out

When your UCAS application is received by the university it will not be on its own but in a batch of, possibly, several hundred. The selectors will have to consider it, along with the others, in between the demands of their 'real' jobs. If your application is uninteresting, lacking evidence of real commitment to physiotherapy or badly worded, it will be put on the reject pile. Nottingham University, for example, receives more than 1,000 applications for its 50 places. From these, about 200 people are interviewed.

Interviews are an essential part of the UCAS process for physiotherapy. You can be called for interview only on the basis of your UCAS application. The selectors will not know about the things that you have forgotten to say and they can get an impression of you only from what is in the application. We have come across too many good students who never got an interview simply because they did not think about the UCAS application; they relied on the hope that the selectors would somehow see through the words and get an instinctive feeling about them. The following sections will tell you more about what the selectors are looking for and how you can avoid common mistakes. Before looking at how the selectors go about deciding whom to call for interview, however, there are a number of important things that you need to think about.

'The best thing about candidates is that they are all different. They are all unique. Therefore our advice is clear; don't write as though you are the same as everyone else. Find the things that are personal to you, your motivations, your values and translate them into your writing. This is our first chance to meet candidates so they need to show their personality. Is the personal statement important? Of course it is. There is a term that we use in application terms: value added. What can this student contribute to the university, the profession and society as a whole. That last point is incredibly important, particularly now as the government changes in the NHS have thrown physiotherapy to the forefront of outreach programmes to promote general health.'

*Admissions tutor*

## The personal statement

This is the most important part of your application, as this is where you convince the selectors that you are a serious and suitable candidate. Advice on writing your personal statement is given in the next chapter.

## The reference

As well as your results and your personal statement, the selectors will take your reference into account. This is where your head, housemaster or housemistress or head of sixth form writes about what an outstanding person you are – the life and soul of the school; how you are on target for three A grades at A level; and why you will become an outstanding physiotherapist. For him or her to say this, of course, it has to be true.

The referee is expected to be as honest as possible and to try to accurately assess your character and potential. You may believe that you have all of the qualities, both academic and personal, necessary in a physiotherapist, but unless you have demonstrated these to your teachers they will be unable to support your application. Ideally, your efforts to impress them will have begun at the start of the sixth form (or before); you will have become involved in school activities, you will have been working hard at your studies and you will be popular with students and teachers alike. However, it is never too late, and some people mature later than others, so if this does not sound like you, start to make efforts now to impress the people who will contribute to your reference.

As part of the reference your referee will need to predict the grades that you are likely to achieve. If your predicted grades are lower than this it is unlikely that you will be considered. Talk to your teachers and find out whether you are on target for these grades. If not, you need to:

- work harder or more effectively – and make sure that your teachers notice that you are doing so, or
- get some extra help either at school or outside, for instance by taking an Easter revision course, or
- delay submitting your UCAS application until you have your A level results. If you decide on this option, make sure that you use your gap year wisely (see below).

## When to submit the UCAS application

The closing date for receipt of the application by UCAS is 6 p.m. on 15 January.

Late applications are accepted by UCAS but the universities are not obliged to consider them. Because of the pressure on places, it is unlikely that late applications will be considered. Although you can submit your application any time between the beginning of September and the January deadline (remembering to get it to your referee at least two weeks before the deadline so that he or she has time to prepare the reference), most admissions tutors admit that the earlier the application is submitted, the better your chance of being called for interview. Your best bet is to talk to the person who will deal with the application in the summer term of your first year of A levels, and work on your personal statement and choice of universities over the summer holidays so that the application is ready to hand in at the start of the September term.

## Deferred entry

Most admissions tutors are happy to consider students who take a gap year, and many encourage it. However, if you are considering this, you need to make sure that you are going to use the time constructively. A year spent watching daytime TV is not going to impress anybody, whereas independent travelling, charity or voluntary work either at home or abroad, work experience or a responsible job will all indicate that you have used the time to develop independence and maturity. Above all, make sure that whatever you do with the year involves regular contact with other people.

You can either apply for deferred entry when you submit your UCAS application, in which case you need to outline your plans in your personal statement, or apply in the September following the publication of your A level results. If you expect to achieve your predicted grades and the feedback from your school or college is that you will be given a good reference, you should apply for deferred entry; but if you are advised by your referee that you are unlikely to be considered, you should give yourself more time to demonstrate to your referees that you have what it takes by waiting until you have your A level results.

## What happens next?

You can follow the progress of your application using the UCAS online track system, which will show you when your form was sent to the universities and their responses.

The next correspondence you will receive, if you are lucky, is likely to be from the universities, asking you to attend an interview. Do not be alarmed if you do not hear anything soon after UCAS has sent you your statement of entry. Some universities interview on a first-come, first-served basis, while others wait until all applications are in before deciding whom to interview.

If you are unlucky you will receive a message from UCAS telling you that you have been rejected by one or more of the universities. Do not despair; you may hear better news from another of the places that you applied to. Even if you get five rejections, the worst thing that you can do is give up and decide that it is no longer worth working hard. On the contrary, if this does happen, you should become even more determined to gain high grades so that you can apply either through Clearing or the following year. The process of making Clearing applications is discussed on page 90.

# 5 | Tweak it
## The personal statement

Be interesting. That is the takeaway message from this chapter. Speak to any admissions tutor and they will tell you that what they want is to read something that maintains their interest. Keep it factual and make it personal. What they are not looking for is a shopping list of your experiences. Look at everything from the point of view of, 'what has this gained me and how has it inspired me to do this course?'.

The personal statement is your opportunity to demonstrate to the selectors that you have not only researched physiotherapy thoroughly, but also have the right personal qualities to succeed as a physiotherapist. There are some universities that do not interview students and therefore they need to see all the information that they are looking for in the personal statement. This chapter will guide you on what you should say and how you should say it.

## Why physiotherapy?

A high proportion of UCAS applications contain the sentence: 'From an early age I have wanted to be a physiotherapist because it is the only career that combines my love of science with the chance to work with people.' Not only do admissions tutors get bored with reading this, but it is also clearly untrue; if you think about it, there are many careers that combine science and people, including teaching, pharmacy, dentistry and nursing. However, the basic ideas behind this sentence may well apply to you.

If so, you need to personalise it. You could mention an incident that first got you interested in physiotherapy – a visit to a physiotherapist, a conversation with a family friend or a lecture at school, for instance. You could write about your interest in human biology, or about a biology project that you undertook when you were younger, to illustrate your interest in science, and you could give examples of how you like to work with others. The important thing is to back up your initial interest in physiotherapy with your efforts to investigate the career.

## What have you done to investigate physiotherapy?

This is the one part that cannot be stressed highly enough. This is where you describe your work experience. It is important to demonstrate that you gained something from the work experience and that it has given you an insight into the profession. You should indicate the length of time that you spent at each work placement, what treatments you observed and your impressions of physiotherapy.

You could comment on what aspects of physiotherapy attract you, what you found interesting or something that surprised you. It is not enough to give details of where you worked and what you saw: the selectors will be asking themselves what you learnt from the experience. Here is an example of a description of work experience that would not impress the selectors.

I spent three days at my local hospital's physiotherapy ward. I saw some patients having ultrasounds, and a man who went in the hydrotherapy pool. It was very interesting.

The next example would be much more convincing because it is clear that the student was interested in what was happening.

During my three weeks at Grantchester General Hospital I was able to shadow two physiotherapists. I watched a range of treatments, including ultrasound and exercise in the hydrotherapy pool. I was particularly interested in the ultrasound treatment because I had only ever seen it used for diagnosis. In the cases that I saw during my work experience it was used to stimulate healing in muscle tissue that had been damaged in an accident. Most of the patients that I saw receiving treatment were elderly. I was able to spend some time with a man who had suffered a stroke and had limited use of his hands. The physiotherapist worked with him on a series of repetitive exercises to try to get him to be able to perform simple tasks. I was also able to see the importance of teamwork because the physiotherapist worked alongside a speech therapist as the man had also lost the ability to communicate effectively.

With luck, the selectors may pick up on this at interview and ask questions about the methods that the physiotherapists used; the student could then bring in his or her knowledge of ultrasound (having investigated it following the work experience). This student would also gain extra credit with the admissions tutors for having arranged length-ier work experience placements.

## Personal qualities

As a physiotherapist you will be working with others throughout your career. To qualify as a physiotherapist you will study alongside maybe 30 others in your year, for three years.

> **TIP!**
>
> The person reading your UCAS application has to decide two things: whether you have the right personal qualities to become a success-ful physiotherapist, and whether you will cope with and contribute to university life.

To be a successful physiotherapist you need to be able to relate to other people; to survive and enjoy university you need to be able to get on with a wide range of people too. Unlike school life, where many of the activi-ties are organised and arranged by the teachers, almost all of the social activities at university are instigated and organised by the students. For this reason the selectors are looking for people who have the enthusiasm and ability to motivate others and are prepared to give up their own time to arrange sporting, dramatic, musical or social activities.

It is also important to mention manual dexterity. Do you have any particular skills that show this, for example: playing a musical instru-ment; juggling; origami? Essentially, anything goes provided it shows your dexterous ability. After all, this is a career that involves you using your hands!

## Extracurricular activities

How, then, does the person reading your personal statement know whether you have the qualities that they are looking for? They will expect to read about some of the following:

- participation in team events
- involvement in school plays or concerts
- positions of responsibility
- work in the local community
- part-time or holiday jobs
- charity work.

The selectors will be aware that some schools offer more in the way of activities and responsibilities than others, and they will make allowances for this. You do not have to have gone on a school expedition to India or to be head girl to be considered, but you need to be able to demonstrate that you have taken the best possible advantage of what is on offer. The selectors will be aware of the type of school or college that you have come from (there is a box on the back of the UCAS application that your referee fills in) and, consequently, of the opportunities that are open to you. What they are looking for is that you have grasped these opportunities.

## General tips

- Do not attempt to copy passages from other sources and incorporate them into your personal statement. UCAS uses anti-plagiarism software when checking statements; if you have used material from someone else (including the examples in this book), you will be caught out and your application will be void.
- Do not be tempted to get someone else (a friend, teacher, parent or one of the many internet sites that offer 'help') to write your personal statement. It has to sound like you, which is why it is called a personal statement.
- Although you can apply for up to five institutions or courses, you write only one personal statement, and so it needs to be relevant to all of the courses you are applying for. You will not be able to write a convincing statement if you are applying to a variety of different courses.
- Print off a copy of your personal statement so that you can remind yourself of all the wonderful things you said, should you be called for interview!
- If you are applying for deferred entry, state your reasons for doing so and outline what you intend to do during your gap year. For example, you might be planning to find some relevant work experience in a private practice, and then spend some time overseas volunteering with children.
- Do not be tempted to use overly formal or long-winded English.
- Read through a draft of your statement and ask yourself: 'Does it sound like me?' If not, rewrite it.
- Avoid phrases such as 'I was fortunate enough to be able to shadow a physiotherapist ...' when you really mean 'I shadowed a physiotherapist ...' or 'I arranged to shadow a physiotherapist ...'

## First sample personal statement

I first became interested in becoming a physiotherapist following treatment for a knee injury. This interest was confirmed after attending a seminar given to our school science society on biomechanics, and by undertaking several work experience placements. In my local hospital I worked alongside physiotherapists on a neurological rehabilitation ward and was able to observe hydrotherapy treatment and also the treatment of children with cystic fibrosis. I helped with a wide range of exercise programmes both in and out of the hydrotherapy pool, and have benefited from the training on subjects that are relevant to children. I have also been involved in teaching swimming to children with learning disabilities and visiting elderly people. This range of experience has helped me to understand the differing demands placed on therapists, the importance of mutual trust and teamwork, and the place of physiotherapy within healthcare. Pain management and biomechanics are also areas that I'm genuinely enthralled by and find absorbing. I believe this interest will be vital when studying physiotherapy as it will help with diagnosing the cause of injury, and it will provide the mechanical basis for taping techniques, braces and orthotic devices. Biomechanics may also guide me in prescribing specific rehabilitation and indicate what exercises certain individuals should avoid.

I have a part-time job in my local supermarket dealing with customer enquiries. I found this stressful at first because almost everyone I had to deal with wanted to complain about something! But I soon learnt how to defuse the situation and to help them to sort out their problems by remaining calm and polite and by listening to what they had to say. I think that this has helped me in my voluntary work as well. I chose physics and sociology at A level, alongside biology, because they will help me when I study physiotherapy at university. Physics helps me to develop my problem-solving skills as well as my understanding of the mechanics of movement, and sociology deals with important issues such as health and illness. Sociology has given me an insight into people and behavioural science. In my opinion, I feel that sociological theories and studies form the basis of many academic studies.

I participate in many sports, am captain of the school A team for netball and have also played for the 1st XI hockey team. Consequently I understand the dynamics of a team and can be both a team member and leader; useful traits when working in a busy physiotherapy department. I enjoy textiles and have made several rugs and items of clothing. I like photography, particularly the work of Ansel Adams, who photographed landscapes, and his work has inspired me to go to a number of national parks to take pictures. Looking at Da Vinci's drawings on the human body as well has inspired me to greater understand how muscles work. I go to the cinema and theatre as often as I can and I like music. I have taken grade 7 clarinet and am learning the guitar, which I play badly in a band that I formed with some friends. We have yet to play in public! This has, however, developed manual dexterous skills that will be useful to manipulate patients' bodies. For my gap year I have arranged to spend six months working in a school for children with serious physical disabilities, and I will then travel with friends to India, Thailand and Vietnam.

I look forward to the challenge of an intensive degree in physiotherapy. I believe that I have the attributes and skills to make a huge contribution to both the academic and communal aspects of university life.

## Second sample personal statement

My interest in physiotherapy developed while giving follow-up treatment to my horse after he was seen by an equine physiotherapist. Through getting this hands-on experience doing stretches and exercises with him, I was able to see improvements in his movement and this fuelled my fascination with physiotherapy. By undertaking work experience and talking to physiotherapists in different fields, I have confirmed that physiotherapy is what I want to do.

During my week at Hobbs Rehabilitation, a neurological rehabilitation clinic, I observed a range of treatments in the gyms and hydrotherapy pool. Of particular interest was the use of the pool in the treatment of patients who had experienced a stroke or suffered from conditions such as cerebral palsy. The water allowed them to gain a much greater range of movement and I was interested to see how each set of exercises was adapted to the individual through the use of equipment, such as floats. I saw how physiotherapists and occupational therapists work together to achieve a common goal for a patient, such as being able to move around the house.

I also spent time at Musgrove Park Hospital, where I was able to follow physiotherapists on different wards (care of the elderly, respiratory, neurological and vascular surgery) and in outpatients. I particularly enjoyed my time on the respiratory ward, as I was able to learn about the role of a physiotherapist in situations such as critical care. This is something I am looking forward to studying further in the cardio-respiratory module. Throughout my time there I was able to observe how the doctors, nurses, physiotherapists and occupational therapists work together in a hospital environment and the teamwork required to return a patient to full health.

Last year I completed my A levels in biology and geography, achieving A* grades. Studying biology has given me a greater understanding of bodily processes. This will give me a good basis for theory modules on the course and help me with the practical placements. Geography has allowed me to study many social aspects of world issues, as well as how the environment affects health.

In addition to completing my A level Chemistry this year, I am also volunteering at a local nursing home once a week. Already this has given me an insight into the needs of the elderly and has greatly humbled me to see how much a simple gesture can mean so much to the residents. Throughout the year I have also arranged more work experience placements, to gain a fuller understanding of the breadth of the physiotherapy profession.

I have learnt skills necessary for the profession through a range of other experiences and believe each to be a valuable tool for a physiotherapist. In 2010 I went to Australia for a school year. This was an outward-bound year where outdoor activities were combined with school in a remote setting. During my last six-day hike I took the role of both leader and group member, which deepened my understanding of the importance of being able to be both. This overseas experience also developed my self-reliance and my ability to problem solve, as many challenges presented themselves throughout the year and I had no direct communication with home.

In 2012 I went to Sri Lanka to work in an area affected by the 2004 tsunami. While I was there I taught English to a large class at a local primary school. There was no interpreter and none of the children spoke any English. I feel the skills I learnt will be very useful when treating the range of patients a physiotherapist treats, especially those who have trouble communicating. Through my main hobby of horse riding I have developed manual dextrous skills and the ability to feel and adapt, which will be useful to manipulate bodies when treating a patient.

I aim to be an excellent physiotherapist. I look forward to developing the specific knowledge and skills, building on the sound foundation that I believe I have already developed.

# 6 | At full stretch
## The interview

If the selectors like the picture that the UCAS application has painted of you they may call you for interview. The purpose of the interview is to allow them to see whether this picture is an accurate one and to investigate whether you have a genuine interest in physiotherapy. You must be aware of current events in the profession; this is discussed in Chapter 7. The interviewers will generally ask you three types of question:

1. those designed to relax you so that they can assess your communication skills
2. those designed to investigate your interest in and suitability for physiotherapy
3. those designed to get a clearer picture of your personal qualities.

Sometimes the question will be no harder than 'Why this university?' However, that can catch many out, so make sure you have done even the basic research before your interview.

## Questions to get you relaxed

### 'How was your journey here today?'

The interviewers are not really interested in the details of your travel. Do not be tempted to give them a minute-by-minute account of your bus journey ('... and then we waited for six minutes at the road works on Corporation Street ...'), but also do not simply say 'OK'. Say something like: 'It was fine, thank you. The train journey took about two hours, which gave me the chance to catch up on some reading.' With a bit of luck they will ask you what you read, which gives you the chance to talk about a book, newspaper article or an item in *Frontline*.

### 'I am interested to know why you decided to apply to Grantchester.'

Another variation on this might be: 'How did you narrow your choice down to five universities?' The panel will be looking for evidence of research and that your reasons are based on informed judgement.

Probably the best possible answer would start with 'I came to your open day ...', because you can then proceed to tell them why you like their university so much, what impressed you about the course and facilities and how the atmosphere of the place would particularly suit you. Even if you are unable to attend open days, try to arrange a formal or informal visit before you are interviewed so that you can show that you are aware of the environment, both academic and physical, and that you like the place. If you know people who are at the university or on the course, so much the better.

You should also know about the course structure. On pages 20–22 there is an overview of the differences and similarities between courses, and the prospectus will give detailed information. Given the choice between a candidate who is not only going to make a good physiotherapist but clearly wants to come to their institution, and another who may have the right qualities but does not seem to care whether he or she studies there or somewhere else, whom do you think the selectors will choose?

Answers to avoid include the following:

- 'Reputation' (unless you know in detail the areas for which the university is highly regarded).
- 'It's in London, and I don't want to move away from my friends.'
- 'You take a lot of retake students.'
- 'My dad says it is easy to get a place here.'

A good answer could be: 'I came to an open day last summer, which is why I have applied here. I enjoyed the day, and was impressed by the facilities, and by the comments of the students who showed us around because they seemed so enthusiastic about the course. Also, my cousin studied English at the university and I visited her, and got to sample the atmosphere of the town.'

There are variations on this question. The interviewers may ask you what you know about the course, or about the university. In all cases, this is your chance to show the interviewers that you are desperate to come to their university.

---

**WARNING!**

Do your homework by reading the prospectus and looking at the website. Although on the surface all physiotherapy courses appear to cover broadly the same subjects, there are big differences in how the courses are delivered and in the opportunities for patient contact, and your interviewers will expect you to know about their course.

# Questions about physiotherapy

### 'Why do you want to be a physiotherapist?'

This is the question that all interviewees expect. Given that the interviewers will be aware that you are expecting the question, they will also expect your answer to be planned carefully. If you look surprised, and say something like 'Um ... well ... I haven't really thought about why ...', you can expect to be rejected. Other answers to avoid are: 'The money'; 'I couldn't get into medicine'; 'I want to help people'; 'I want to work for Arsenal'.

Many students are worried that they will sound insincere when they answer this question. The way to avoid this is to try to bring in reasons that are personal to you, for instance an incident that started your interest (perhaps a visit to a physiotherapist), or an aspect of your work experience that particularly fascinated you. The important thing is to try to express clearly what interested you rather than to generalise your answers. Rather than say 'Physiotherapy combines science, working with people and the chance to have control over your career', which says little about you, tell the interviewers about the way in which your interest progressed. Here is an example of a good answer.

'Although it seemed strange to my friends, I used to enjoy going with my grandfather to a physiotherapist when he had difficulty in walking due to arthritis. This was because the physiotherapist explained things very clearly and patiently, and I was interested in what was happening around me. My favourite subject is biology, particularly the anatomy side of it, and I always wanted to do something that involved this. When I was thinking about my career I arranged to shadow a physiotherapist, and the more time I spent at the hospital the more I realised that this would really suit me. This also gave me the chance to find out about what being a physiotherapist is really like. The things about physiotherapy that I particularly enjoy are ...'

### WARNING!

Do not learn this passage and repeat it at your interview. Ensure that your answer is not only personal to you, but also honest.

With luck, the interviewers will pick up on something that you said about work experience and ask you more questions about this. Since 'Why do you want to be a physiotherapist?' is such an obvious question, interviewers often try to find out the information in different ways. Expect questions such as 'When did your interest in physiotherapy start?', 'What was it about your work experience that finally convinced you that physiotherapy was for you?' or 'I see that you spent two weeks with your physiotherapist. Was there anything that surprised you?'

Variations on this question could include 'Was there anything that particularly interested you?', 'Was there anything you found off-putting?' or simply 'Tell me about your work experience'. What these questions really mean is: 'Are you able to show us that you were interested in what was happening during your work experience?' To return to the original question, answering either 'Yes' or 'No' without explanation will not gain you many marks. Similarly, saying 'Yes, I was surprised by the number of patients who seemed very scared' says nothing about your awareness of the physiotherapist's approach to his or her patients.

However, answering 'Yes, I was surprised by the number of patients who seemed very scared. What struck me, however, was the way in which the physiotherapist dealt with each patient as an individual, sometimes being sympathetic, sometimes explaining things in great detail and sometimes using humour to relax them. For instance ...' shows that you were interested enough to be aware of more than the most obvious things.

Sentences that start with 'For example ...' and 'For instance...' are particularly important, as they allow you to demonstrate your interest. In order to be able to give examples, you should keep a diary of things that you saw during your work experience so that you do not forget. You should read through this before your interview, as if you were revising for an examination.

### 'I see that you try to keep up to date with developments in physiotherapy. Can you tell me about something that you have read about recently?'

If you are interested in making physiotherapy your career, the selectors will expect you to be interested enough in the subject to want to read about it. Good sources of information are the CSP's website and others (addresses are given in Chapter 11), *Frontline* and the national newspapers. You should get into the habit of looking at a broadsheet newspaper every day to see if there are any medical or physiotherapy-related stories.

Note that the question uses the word 'recently': recent does not mean an article you read two years ago – keep up to date. You could, for instance, say: 'There was a recent report that sportspeople risk injury from wearing air-filled training shoes. There was a survey of basketball players that showed that they were four times more likely to suffer ankle injuries if they were wearing trainers with soles that contained air pockets.'

**'During your work experience, you had the chance to discuss physiotherapy with physiotherapists. What do you know about career opportunities and pay for physiotherapists?'**

You must make sure that you do some research on career paths by asking questions about this when you meet physiotherapists.

Most physiotherapists work in the NHS, but there are many other options. On pages 7–11 we described many of the types of work undertaken by physiotherapists. Most physiotherapists end up specialising in one or more particular areas – in most cases as a result of an interest that grew during their training. The best answer to a question like this is to describe the career paths of physiotherapists you have met and worked with, as this will allow you to highlight your own work experience.

**'What qualities should a physiotherapist possess?'**

These have been discussed on page 51. However, do not simply list them. The question has not been asked because the interviewer is puzzled about what these qualities are; it has been asked to give you a chance to show:

- that you are aware of them, and
- that you possess them.

The best way to answer this is to use phrases such as 'During my work experience at the Grantchester Physiotherapy Clinic I was able to observe/talk to the physiotherapist, and I became aware that …', or 'Communication is very important. For instance, when I was shadowing my physiotherapist, there was a patient who …' Try always to relate these general questions to your own experiences.

**'Physiotherapy requires high levels of physical fitness and manual dexterity. Do you possess these?'**

Manual manipulation of a patient's limbs requires a fair degree of fitness and strength, and as a physiotherapist you will need to be able to help to lift and lower patients. If you have trouble picking up a coffee cup without breathing heavily for the next 10 minutes, physiotherapy may not be the best career for you. The interviewers will need to be reassured that you are able to work in a physically demanding environment, and also that you have the manual dexterity necessary to perform sometimes intricate tasks. Try to anticipate this question by preparing an answer that demonstrates that you have these qualities. Sport is always a good indicator of fitness and coordination, but you could also mention situations that you encountered during your work experience, demanding tasks that you perform as part of a weekend job, expeditions that you have been on at school as part of the Duke of Edinburgh's Award, or a hobby such as DIY.

> **WARNING!**
>
> Do not lie about the example you describe. An admissions tutor I talked to recounted the story of an applicant who wrote in the UCAS application that he worked for a local Riding for the Disabled scheme. However, the previous interview had been with someone from the same town who had explained that there was no such scheme in the area, which is why she could not carry on doing this when she moved there. He was found out, and rejected.

## Questions to find out about what sort of person you are

### 'What do you do to relax?'

Do not say 'watch TV' or 'go to the pub'. Mention something that involves working or communicating with others, for instance sport or music. Use the question to demonstrate that you possess the qualities required in a physiotherapist. However, do not make your answer so insincere that the interviewers realise that you are trying to impress them. Saying 'I relax most effectively when I go to the local physiotherapy clinic to shadow the physiotherapist' will not convince them.

### 'How do you cope with stress?'

Physiotherapy can be a stressful occupation. Physiotherapists have to deal with difficult people, those who are scared and those who react badly when in a physiotherapy ward. For many people, physiotherapy can be painful and distressing and patients are not always cooperative, or even aware of why they are receiving treatment. In these circumstances the physiotherapist cannot panic, but must remain calm and rational. The interviewers will want to make a judgement as to whether you will be able to cope with the demands of the job.

Having been through them themselves, it is unlikely that they will regard school examinations as being particularly stressful. Hard work, yes, but not as stressful as training to be a physiotherapist or practising as a physiotherapist. What they are looking for are answers that demonstrate your calmness and composure when dealing with others. You could relate it to your work experience, or your Saturday job. Dealing with a queue of angry and impatient customers demanding to know why their cheeseburgers are not ready can be difficult. Other areas that can provide evidence of stress management are school expeditions, public speaking or positions of responsibility at school or outside.

**'I see that you enjoy reading. What is the most recent book that you have read?'**

The question might be about the cinema or theatre, but the point of it is the same: to get you talking about something that interests you. Although it may sound obvious, if you have written in your UCAS application that you enjoy reading, make sure that you have actually read something recently. Admissions tutors will be able to tell you stories about interviewees who look at them with absolute amazement when they are asked about books, despite it featuring in the personal statement.

Answers such as 'Well ... I haven't had much time recently, but ... let me see ... I read *Elle* last month, and ... oh yes ... I had to read *Jane Eyre* for my English GCSE' will do your chances no good at all. By all means put down that you like reading, but make sure that you have read an interesting novel in the period leading up to the interview, and be prepared to discuss it.

# How to succeed in your interview

You should prepare for an interview as if you are preparing for an examination. This involves revision of your work experience diary so that you can recount details of your time with physiotherapists, revision of the newspaper, website and *Frontline* articles that you have saved, and revision of all of the things that you have mentioned on your personal statement.

> *'I was nervous in my interview and I misunderstood the question I was asked about what it is like to be a physiotherapist. However, they were very reassuring and allowed me an opportunity to think around the question. I got my place, so it just goes to show that they are not trying to catch you out in an interview, they just want to see what you know.'*
>
> Giles, University of Liverpool

When you are preparing for your A levels you sit a mock examination so that the real thing does not come as a total surprise; when you are preparing for an interview, have a mock interview so that you can get some feedback on your answers. Your school may be able to help you. If not, independent sixth-form colleges usually provide a mock interview service. Friends of your parents may also be able to help. If possible, video your mock interview so that you are aware of the way you come across in an interview situation. There is a list of practice interview questions below.

## Mock interview questions

- Why do you want to be a physiotherapist?
- What have you done to investigate physiotherapy?
- Why does physiotherapy interest you more than medicine/nursing/radiography?
- What are the ideal qualities that a physiotherapist should possess?
- Do you possess these qualities?
- Give me an example of how you cope with stress.
- Why did you apply to this university?
- Did you come to our open day?
- During your work experience, did anything surprise you?
- During your work experience, did anything shock you?
- Was the physiotherapist you shadowed good at communicating with his/her patients?
- Tell me about preventive physiotherapy.
- What is occupational therapy?
- What is repetitive strain injury?
- What is cystic fibrosis/a stroke/arthritis?
- What is hydrotherapy?
- What is ultrasound and how is it used?
- Is exercise always good for you?
- How much do NHS physiotherapists earn?
- Have you read any articles about physiotherapy recently?
- What advances can we expect in physiotherapy technology/treatment in the future?
- What have you done to demonstrate your commitment to the community?
- What would you contribute to this university?
- What are your best/worst qualities?
- What was the last novel you read? What did you think of it?
- What was the last play/film you saw? What did you think of it?
- What do you do to relax?
- What is your favourite A level subject?
- What grades do you expect to gain in your A levels?
- What precautions need to be taken with patients who are HIV positive?
- How does teamwork apply to the role of a physiotherapist?
- What branch of physiotherapy interests you the most, and why?
- What is the role of a physiotherapist in a hospital?
- Why are communication skills important for physiotherapists?
- What have you done that demonstrates your communication skills?
- What have you done that demonstrates your leadership skills?
- What have you done that demonstrates your ability to cope in a stressful situation?
- Why is a knowledge of physics helpful in physiotherapy?

- What are the particular difficulties that animal physiotherapists encounter?
- How did you organise your work experience?
- Why are you taking a gap year?

## MMIs

There is a growing use of MMIs (Multiple Mini Interviews) being used now at the application stage. The School of Healthcare Sciences at Cardiff University, for example, uses eight mini interviews, each lasting five minutes in length, in order to get candidates to think on their feet. They provide the following guidance on the purpose and usage of the interview technique:

'The MMI stations assess the ability to apply general knowledge to issues relevant to the culture and society in which students will be. Equally important will be the assessment of the ability to communicate and articulate personal opinions. It is important to know that there are no right answers for many of the MMI scenarios and that it is not intended to test the amount of prior knowledge in these domains.

The stations have been carefully designed to assess the following attributes:

- Motivation to become a physiotherapist
- Everyone counts: Care and Compassion
- Working together using initiative, problem solving and team work
- Respect for privacy and dignity
- Commitment to quality of care
- Reflection on a learning experience
- Promoting and improving quality of life
- Following written and verbal instructions.'*

*Information taken from www.cardiff.ac.uk/study/undergraduate/ applying/admissions-criteria/physiotherapy, with kind permission from The School of Healthcare Sciences at Cardiff University.

If you are going to be having an MMI then it would be a good idea to ask multiple members of staff at your school to ask you different questions and get you to think on your feet.

### Sample MMI questions

Station #1:

PROMPT (Read and consider for 2 minutes):

A friend tells you that her dad has been battling alcoholism for years and it has put a strain on the family. They are thinking they will have to leave their studies and go home to help out in the family as it is all too much right now. How do you counsel your friend?

RESPOND: (Speak max. 8 minutes)

### Station #2:

PROMPT (Read and consider for 2 minutes):

What do you think are the major sorts of problems facing a person with a long-term health problem, such as arthritis?

RESPOND: (Speak max. 8 minutes)

### Station #3:

PROMPT (Read and consider for 2 minutes):

Imagine you are on a committee able to recommend only one of two new treatments to be made available through the NHS. The treatments are: an artificial heart for babies born with heart defects, or a permanent replacement hip for people with severe arthritis. Both treatments are permanent, i.e. never need repeating, and are of equal cost. On what grounds would you make your arguments?

RESPOND: (Speak max. 8 minutes)

### Station #4:

PROMPT (Read and consider for 2 minutes):

Can you think of something you'd like to invent?

RESPOND: (Speak max. 8 minutes)

### Station #5:

PROMPT (Read and consider for 2 minutes):

Give us an example of something about which you used to hold strong opinions, but have had to change your mind. What made you change? What do you think now?

RESPOND: (Speak max. 8 minutes)

## Appearance and body language

Appearance and body language are important. The impression you create can be very influential. Remember that if the interviewers cannot picture you as a physiotherapist in future years they are unlikely to offer you a place.

## Body language

- Maintain eye contact with the interviewers.
- Direct most of what you are saying to the person who asked you the question, but occasionally look around at the others on the panel.
- Sit up straight, but adopt a position that you feel comfortable in.
- Do not wave your hands around too much, but do not keep them gripped together to stop them moving. Fold them across your lap, or rest them on the arms of the chair.

## Speech

- Talk slowly and clearly.
- Do not use slang.
- Avoid saying 'erm ...', 'you know' or 'sort of'.
- Say 'hello' at the start of the interview, and 'thank you' and 'goodbye' at the end.

## Dress and appearance

- Wear clothes that show you have made an effort for the interview.
- You do not have to wear a business suit, but a jacket and tie (men) or a skirt and blouse (women) are appropriate.
- Make sure that you are clean and tidy.
- If appropriate, shave before the interview (but avoid overpowering aftershave).
- Clean your nails and shoes.
- Wash your hair.
- Avoid (visible) piercings, earrings (men), jeans and trainers.

## At the end of the interview

You may be given the opportunity to ask a question at the end of the interview. Bear in mind that the interviews are carefully timed, and that your attempts to impress the panel with 'clever' questions may do quite the opposite. The golden rule is: ask a question only if you are genuinely interested in the answer (which, of course, you were unable to find during your careful reading of the prospectus).

## Questions to avoid

- What is the structure of the first year of the course?
- Will I be able to live in a hall of residence?
- When will I first have contact with patients?

As well as being boring questions, the answers to these will be available in the prospectus. You have obviously not done any serious research.

### Questions you could ask

- 'Are my A levels enough of a foundation before starting this course or could you recommend something else I should review before starting.' Proactive.
- 'Do you think I should try to get more work experience before the start of the course?' Again, an indication of your keenness.
- 'Earlier, I couldn't answer the question you asked me on ultrasound. What is the answer?' Something that you genuinely might want to know.
- 'How soon will you let me know if I have been successful or not?' Something you really want to know.

---

### REMEMBER!

If in doubt, do not ask a question. End by saying 'All of my questions have been answered by the prospectus and the students who showed me around the university. Thank you very much for an interesting day.' Smile, shake hands (if appropriate – if you are being interviewed by a panel of five, who are all sitting at the other end of a long table, then do not!) and say goodbye.

---

## Structuring the interview

The selectors will have a set of questions that they may ask, designed to assess your suitability and commitment. If you answer 'Yes' or 'No' to most questions, or reply only in monosyllables, they will fire more and more questions at you. If, however, your answers are longer and also contain statements that interest them, they are more likely to pick up on these and you are, effectively, directing the interview. If you are asked questions that you have prepared for there will be less time for the interviewers to ask you questions that might be more difficult to answer.

For example, at the end of your answer to a question about work experience, you might say '... and the physiotherapist was able to explain the effect of new technology on physiotherapy.' The interviewer may then say: 'I see. Can you tell me about how technology is changing physiotherapy?' You can then embark on an answer about ultrasound, for instance. At the end of your explanation you could finish with: '... of course, ultrasound treatment is often used in conjunction with infrared radiation treatment.' You might then be asked about situations where this might happen, and so on.

Of course, this does not always work, but you would be very unlucky not to have at least one of these 'signposts' followed that you placed in front of the interviewers.

# How you are selected

During the interview the panel will be assessing you in various categories. Whether or not the interview appears to be structured, the interviewers will be following careful guidelines so that they can compare candidates from different interview sessions. Some panels adopt a conversational style, whereas others are more formal. The scoring system will vary from place to place but, in general, you will be assessed in the following categories:

- reason for your choice of university
- academic ability
- motivation for physiotherapy
- awareness of physiotherapy issues
- personal qualities
- communication skills.

You are likely to be scored in each category, and the university will have a minimum mark that you will have to gain if you are to be made an offer. If you are below this score, but close to it, you may be put on an official or unofficial waiting list. If this happens you may be considered in August, should there be places available.

If you are offered a place you will receive a letter from the university telling you what you need to achieve in your A levels. This is called a conditional offer. Post-A level students who have achieved the necessary grades will be given unconditional offers. If you are unlucky, all you will get is an email from UCAS saying that you have been rejected. If this happens it is not necessarily the end of the road that leads you to a career in physiotherapy.

If you are rejected by all of your choices, you can enter the UCAS Extra scheme, which allows you to contact other universities. If you still are without a place when the A level results are released in August, you will be eligible to apply for vacant places through Clearing.

When UCAS has received replies from all of your choices it will send you a Statement of Offers. You will then have about a month to make up your mind about where you want to go. If you have only one offer you will have little choice but to accept it. If you have more than one you will have to accept one as your firm choice and another (usually a lower offer) as your insurance choice. If the place where you really want to study makes a lower offer than one of your other choices, do not be tempted to choose the lower offer as your insurance choice, since you will be obliged to go to the university that you have put as your firm choice if you achieve the grades. Even if you narrowly miss the grade, you may still be accepted by your first choice. If you decide that you do not want to go there, once the results are issued, you will have to withdraw from the UCAS system for that year.

# 7| Do you know your gluteus maximus from your articulatio cubiti?
## Current issues

This chapter explains the most relevant current issues in physiotherapy. This should be used as a reference point for your interview but not as your only source of information. You should make sure that you read newspapers and journals (such as *Frontline*) to get ideas on other current issues and not just rely on those listed here. Your success at interview will depend on your ability to converse fluently on up-to-date topics. You do not have to be an expert in your field – that is what the interviewers are – but you do need to have tried to understand the profession that you wish to follow. If that comes as a surprise, this is not the right career for you!

## Financial pressures threatening NHS Scotland's physiotherapy services

According to Scotland's spending watchdog, Audit Scotland, the NHS is unable to continue providing current physiotherapy services as budget cuts and rising demand have meant a problem in the supply and retention of physiotherapists. The CSP Scotland has said that there needs to be investment in order to improve services.

In 2014/15, £11.4 billion was spent by health boards and many needed government help to break even. All boards fell short of national target budgets. As of March 2015, only two key waiting time targets were met out of a possible nine.

The CSP believes that the pressures on the services are set to increase in the future and that physiotherapy services are vulnerable to cuts, despite the profession being responsible for preventing long hospital waiting lists. Temporary staffing cost 15 per cent more than the previous year at £284 million last year as there is not only a problem recruiting but also retaining permanent staff.

The CSP is focusing its messaging ahead of Scottish parliamentary elections on encouraging investment in order to reinvigorate physiotherapy services in Scotland.

# Concussion

The Rugby World Cup did not just bring fantastic sporting drama to our shores. It also increased awareness on a serious issue that has been more and more in the spotlight over the past year: concussion. Professional sportsmen and women are under increasing risk of head injuries nowadays as sport is getting more physical with increased training regimes to blame for the development of size and strength.

## Clinical update: Concussion

According to a report in the CSP's *Frontline* magazine, minor head trauma isn't just a sports injury:

'Physios in all specialisms can help to spot undiagnosed concussion that needs treatment.

Concussion is a minor traumatic brain injury caused by a blow to the head or violent head movement, such as in a traffic collision. Although there is often no outward damage, and the patient usually stays conscious, the jolt may briefly disrupt electrical activity in the brain.

It's more common among sports players, young men, older people and those who are homeless or have mental health problems. Children and teenagers take longer to recover and are more likely to suffer long-term damage. Having concussion more than once increases the risk of long-term damage.

Among sports players, evidence suggests that women are more likely to have concussion, and that the risk may be related to the menstrual cycle, with experts noting that sportswomen often recover slower from concussion than sportsmen.

Anyone suffering a head injury should be monitored over several days as bleeding inside the skull is not immediately obvious.

In sport, there are new laws around head injuries. Any head injury should be treated as serious and the player be immediately removed from the field of play and not allowed to return during the match. They should then be properly medically assessed. There should be a minimum period of one week's rest and then the Graduated Return To Play programme is applied, once the symptoms have stopped. This is a minimum of one week and they need to be carefully monitored by medical staff and physiotherapists.'*

*Information taken from the CSP (www.csp.org.uk), with kind permission from the CSP.

### The role of a physiotherapist

All physiotherapists in any field have the opportunity to treat and save lives. Any bump on the head could cause minor brain trauma and this could lead to bigger problems in the future. Physiotherapists can pick up on signs or indicators that a patient might be suffering more than they let on, or even perhaps more than they know. A good example in physiotherapy is that of vestibular rehabilitation. This is used in the treatment of a loss of balance but if concussion is involved, the patient may be suffering from other after effects that require looking at and possible treatment.

Symptoms to look out for are: drowsiness, dizziness, nausea, headache or pressure in the head, loss of memory, difficulty in understanding or communicating, sensitivity to light or noise. If they are encountering severe neck pain, deteriorating consciousness, increasing confusion or irritability, severe headache, repeated vomiting, unusual behaviour, convulsions, problems with seeing or hearing or weakness or tingling in arms or legs, then you should seek immediate medical attention.

# Technology in physiotherapy

Enter the words 'physiotherapy' and 'news' into an internet search engine and most of the links that you get are to news stories about new forms of treatment. Although the basic techniques used in physiotherapy have been around for a long time – physical manipulation, repetition of exercises and other forms of manual therapy – technology plays an increasingly important role.

Probably the most widely used application of technology within physiotherapy is ultrasound. Ultrasound treatment utilises high-frequency (up to 3MHz – too high for the human ear to hear) sound waves. Ultrasound is used extensively in medicine for diagnosis, either to form images in order to see what is happening inside the body (for instance, scans that show a foetus inside the womb) or to measure blood flow.

Whenever ultrasound waves pass from one tissue to another, a small percentage of the beam is reflected back, and these reflected sound waves are used to create a picture, or to measure the speed at which blood is flowing (using something called the Doppler effect). Ultrasound can also be used therapeutically; that is, for treatment. It has been used to accelerate tissue repair and to relieve pain since the 1950s. It is used to treat a variety of conditions, such as sports injuries, sprains, tendonitis, arthritis and ulcers, and to relieve the pain associated with, for instance, phantom limbs in amputees. The sound waves penetrate deep into the body and, although the biological effects are not completely understood, it is likely that the vibration caused by the sound waves produces a combination of heating (thermal effects) and stimulation of tissue and blood vessels (mechanical effects). Ultrasound is usually given at the end of a course of treatment, following other forms of manual therapy.

Ultrasound equipment is relatively cheap to buy (less than £2,000 for an ultrasound machine) and is easy to use. The total cost to the NHS of ultrasound in physiotherapy is around £5 million per year – a tiny proportion of the total NHS bill. The drawbacks of the extensive use of ultrasound in physiotherapy are that there is little conclusive clinical evidence that it is effective and that there is a possible risk of tissue damage if the power settings on individual machines are not calibrated accurately.

Another treatment that utilises sound waves, extracorporeal shockwave therapy (ESWT), has been introduced into physiotherapy clinics. ESWT was brought to a wider audience in 2004 when Sachin Tendulkar, the Indian cricketer, received shockwave therapy to treat tennis elbow that had failed to respond to conventional physiotherapy. Developed from the devices that generate pulses of sound waves to destroy kidney stones, ESWT devices produce pulses of high-pressure sound that travel through the skin. Soft tissue and bone that are subjected to these pulses of high-pressure energy heal back stronger. Tennis elbow results from calcification of a tendon and is usually treated with mechanical exercise or steroid injection (which risks weakening the tendon still further), but new treatments are also being developed.

There are instances of robots being used in physiotherapy. This does not mean that next time you require physiotherapy you will be treated by R2-D2, Bender or Kryton. The effective rehabilitation of patients with cerebral palsy, or following a stroke or other brain injuries, requires repetitive movement exercises and controllable resistance to motion. In one such treatment the patient is coupled to a robot joystick that guides him or her through a series of movements. The robot can be programmed to vary the scope of the movement, to increase or decrease the resistance, or to help the patient to complete the movements. To increase interest levels for the patient, the movements can be integrated into a 'game' on a screen in front of the patient. In this way tens of thousands of therapeutic movements can be completed over the course of a few weeks – far more than the physiotherapist could manage, and more than the patient is likely to be able to accomplish alone. Virtual reality is also used to alleviate the boredom often associated with repetitive exercises. Patients can put themselves into a virtual reality environment where they can take part in a game that requires them to perform the necessary therapeutic movements.

In 2015, the new, first all-purpose built Remeo Respiratory unit opened, using state of the art technology, designed to get patients off mechanical ventilation and released from hospital. This is currently allowing physiotherapy rotations with East Surrey Hospital, where it was pioneered.

The newest innovation technologically for physiotherapy is in the presence of apps that are designed to help people to address their physiotherapy issues independently. There is an app that allows you to locate over 100 trigger points in over 70 muscles; there is one that helps you to understand prevention of future medical needs; one that corrects spinal posture; and another that measures range of motion. There are many others as well, that facilitate awareness of your body and give you a feeling of empowerment to treat your body responsibly.

Equally, the rise of social media is having an effect on the profession; specifically Twitter. Physios are now able to tweet exercise tips to a wider audience, ensuring those with low mobility, or simply those with a busy lifestyle, are keeping on top of their fitness.

When discussing technology in physiotherapy, it is also useful to look at the impact of technology on the profession and the amount of injuries caused by poor practice at work with computers and day to day management, all of which will be discussed below.

# An ageing population

It is a well reported fact that the population of the UK is ageing. In fact, Age UK is currently reporting that 11.4 million people in the UK are over 65 years old and 14.9 million over 60 years of age. That means more people are over 60 years old now than under 18 years old. The Office for National Statistics reports that by 2037 a projected one in 10 people will be over 85 and by 2040, 24.2% of the population will be aged over 65 years, compared to 17% in 2010.*

*Information taken from an Age UK factsheet at www.ageuk.org.uk/ Documents/EN-GB/Factsheets/Later_Life_UK_factsheet, with kind permission from Age UK.*

At present, there is a strain on physiotherapy services, which have to deal with the effects of ageing and mobility among the elderly. Physiotherapy services therefore need to focus on facilitating independence among the elderly so that they are not dependent on the health services or care facilities to cope with normal life. Physiotherapy should also enable those still of working age to continue working, thus reducing the need for early retirement. A factsheet on musculoskeletal disorders (MSDs) published by the CSP highlights that MSDs are the most common physiotherapy problem treated among the workforce and are therefore a priority to be addressed in order to prevent further problems down the line.

An article in *Diffusion* (the University of Lancaster's Journal of Undergraduate Research) says that 'being elderly is a state of chronological, sociological and biological ageing' (as determined by Balcombe and Sinclair 2001). This interesting article details how physiotherapy can help, and states that the Health Professions Council (HPC) Standards of

Proficiency for Physiotherapists Standard 3a.1 (2007) 'requires the phys-iotherapist to understand both the development of ageing (physiologically, structurally and behaviourally), and the effect on functional ability'. Never has this been more relevant than at this time, when the NHS is struggling with an ageing population and therefore the clear strategy is to prevent any problems before they occur in the ageing population, thus reducing reliance on the health service.

You can find the *Diffusion* article at http://bcur.org/journals/index.php/ Diffusion/article/view/167/148.

A further pressure resulting from an ageing population is a rise in the number of incidents of chronic obstructive pulmonary disease (COPD) and strokes (CfWI, 2010). Working as members of a multidisciplinary team, physiotherapists need to help with the rehabilitation of such patients while they are in hospital.

## Obesity

Obesity is one of the biggest health challenges that we face in this country. It is an issue that the government is now actively trying to com-bat, as 26% of adults in the UK are currently obese. Statistics from the Department of Health and Foresight report indicated that if the trend continues, then by 2050, nine in 10 adults will be overweight. While this is roughly still the case, recent modelling has shown that by 2030, 41% to 48% of men and 38% to 43% of women will be obese. The annual cost to the NHS is roughly £4.2 billion (estimated to be £9.7 billion by 2050); and the cost to the wider economy is £49.9 billion.

As we have already discussed, prevention is just as important as cure. Working alongside other schemes such as the healthy-eating Change 4Life movement, which gained prominence during the London 2012 Olympic and Paralympic Games, the CSP is currently targeting the obesity issue with the Move for Health campaign, which encourages the public to take control of their health and well-being by engaging in regular exercise. The CSP recommends that an adult should exercise five times a week at moderate intensity for roughly 30 minutes. If that is not physically possible, i.e. you have time constraints that do not allow a concentrated period of exercise, then manage your time effectively and split the 30 minutes into shorter sessions at different intervals throughout the day. It may sound obvious, but this will have a positive effect on your health if continued over a long period of time.

The campaign is designed to show people that increased levels of physical activity can prevent, or help to control, more than 20 medical conditions, most notably obesity, osteoarthritis, heart disease, type 2 diabetes and other conditions affecting well-being such as depression. If nothing else, the release of endorphins through increased levels of activity will have a positive effect on productivity and output during a working day. It is a complete endorsement of the adage 'healthy body, healthy mind'.

### Childhood obesity

Childhood obesity is a topic that remains a major concern; however, the NHS reports that the rate is stabilising. Schoolgirl Martha Payne brought this debate very much to the fore in 2012 when she blogged about her school lunches. The issue of childhood obesity is particularly important in terms of preventing our children from becoming obese and protecting future generations. There has been a four-fold increase in childhood obesity in recent years. As recently as August 2013, the media reported that 30% of children in the UK were obese.

The statistics are compelling, the most shocking being that a quarter of children aged two to 15 years spend at least six hours every weekend day being inactive. This is the highest rate in Western Europe. In order to address the dangers that obesity can pose for children's health, a scheme similar to its older sibling is being run by the CSP. Working alongside the British Dietetic Association, the Move for Health Kids campaign recommends that children should exercise for at least an hour every day. Would you have known that Jamie Oliver and physiotherapists are so hand in hand?

# Parkinson's disease

The international guidelines for physiotherapists who treat patients with Parkinson's disease have now been adapted for use in the UK.

Following the research and evidence-based work that was done by the Royal Dutch Society for Physical Therapy, the Parkinson's Disease Society set up a project to make these guidelines accessible for clinical use in the UK. One of the main innovative features of the guidelines is that they include four 'quick reference' cards to be used in clinical practice, whether in clinics, on wards or in the community. These relate to best practice for Parkinson's disease in the diagnosis of it:

● QRC 1: History taking
● QRC 2: Physical examination
● QRC 3: Specific treatment and goals
● QRC 4: Treatment strategies

They have been designed to each fit on a single side of A4 and are to be placed in an open area that can be accessed by physiotherapists.

These guidelines are an update of those published by the National Institute for Health and Clinical Excellence in 2006. Physiotherapists have emphasised their relevance to the profession because they focus on areas that involve the physiotherapist, such as assessment, treatment and outcome measurement, as opposed to the strictly medicine-based approach of doctors.

# Repetitive strain injury

Repetitive strain injury (RSI) is an increasingly common complaint among computer users. As the name suggests, the condition is caused by repetition of certain movements, usually associated with computer keyboard use. However, RSI is not confined to computer users and has been diagnosed in many people whose jobs involve manual labour or machine operation. The condition can also occur when the person's posture is inappropriate to the task that he or she is undertaking.

RSI manifests itself as pain, mostly when the task that caused it is being carried out, but often at other times as well. It usually affects the neck, shoulders, elbows, wrists or hands. RSI is also known by other names, including WRMSD (work-related musculoskeletal disorder), WRULD (work-related upper limb disorder), CTD (cumulative trauma disorder) and OOS (occupational overuse syndrome). The term RSI actually encompasses a number of different conditions, most commonly carpal tunnel syndrome. 'Carpal' comes from the Greek word *karpos*, which means wrist. The joint in the wrist is surrounded by fibrous tissue and there is a small gap between this tissue and the bone, through which a nerve (the median nerve) passes. The nerve then splits to serve the fingers and thumb. Repetitive movement of the wrist can cause swelling of the tissue in the wrist, putting pressure on the median nerve. Symptoms include numbness and tingling in the fingers and thumb, followed by pain. The condition can usually be cured by a combination of physiotherapy and rest.

In 2007, the CSP stated that people who work in factories were three times more likely to get RSI than office workers. It said: 'Over 370,000 people in Great Britain are afflicted with RSI and as many as 86,000 new cases were recorded last year. In terms of employee absence, lower productivity and staff turnover, the cost to employers is nearly £300 million!' The Trades Union Congress (TUC) reported that one in 50 workers has RSI and that 5.4 million days were lost in sick leave due to RSI last year. About one third of sufferers are aged under 45 and 55% (276,000) are women. The overall cost to industry is £20 billion. (There is a lack of research to give more up-to-date figures from charities.)

The CSP website reports that the Labour Research Department analysed Health and Safety Executive figures for the CSP and discovered that metal, plastics, textile and other plant and machine workers were the most likely to get RSI (1.1 per 100 workers), followed by bricklayers, plumbers, carpenters and others in skilled trades (0.91 per 100 workers). Professionals (0.32) and managers (0.36) were the least likely to get RSI.

Not everyone believes that RSI actually exists. Carpal tunnel syndrome certainly does, and can be caused by obesity, arthritis, diabetes and pregnancy, but some people are sceptical as to whether repetitive movement is a cause. A report in the *British Medical Journal* on research done at Manchester University cast some doubts on RSI. The research indicated that the majority of those who suffered from arm or wrist pain (105 people in a survey involving 1,200 volunteers) were also the most dissatisfied with their jobs and suffered from high stress levels. In other words, the pain could be due to psychological or stress factors rather than simply the physical aspects of their jobs.

# Rehabilitation of stroke patients

A stroke occurs when a blood clot blocks a blood vessel in the brain, causing brain cells in the area to die. If treatment is not given immediately, further cells in the surrounding areas also die. The functions that were controlled by those brain cells (such as speech, memory or movement) are then affected, depending on the area of the brain where the blood vessels were blocked. The severity of the stroke can vary from patient to patient. The effects may be very minor (and temporary) or they may lead to paralysis or death.

The main types of rehabilitation are:

● physical therapy – to improve mechanical skills such as walking, use of the hands, or balance
● occupational therapy – to re-learn the skills that are required for everyday life such as eating, dressing and looking after oneself
● speech therapy – to re-learn how to communicate effectively.

Physiotherapy for stroke patients must begin as early as possible following the stroke in order to be effective. Improvement is slow and recovery is difficult six months after the stroke. However, paralysed muscles must not be treated too early or they may be damaged permanently.

Research carried out at the University of Texas and reported in *New Scientist* found that rats and monkeys that had received small brain injuries to cause paralysis of a limb suffered further injury if treatment was started immediately. The researchers surmised that glutamate, a neurotransmitter that is released during movement, was the probable cause, since, in large concentrations, it acts as a toxin. Brain damage appeared to multiply its effects. Research is now being carried out to find drugs that will block the effects of glutamate.

The expertise of the physiotherapist is vital in assessing when (and in what form) treatment should start. At the start of the treatment, the physiotherapist will prepare muscles for the more intensive treatments that will follow, and will work on enabling the patient to support his or her own weight if leg muscles are affected. The later stages of physiotherapy may involve compensation for permanently damaged muscles through the introduction of aids such as walking frames. The physiotherapist may work alongside occupational therapists, speech therapists, carers and psychologists to try to prepare the patient for a return to 'normal' life.

## Exercise referral schemes

Introduced 18 years ago, NHS exercise referral schemes have become increasingly popular. In 2004 the government started outlining proposals to provide GPs with national standards for 'prescribing' exercise programmes for their patients.

Exercise referral schemes are used to help patients suffering from a wide range of problems, including:

- coronary heart disease
- diabetes
- hypertension
- mental health problems, including depression
- musculoskeletal problems, e.g. chronic lower-back pain
- obesity
- problems caused by falls.

In the 10-year review in July 2004, the CSP published figures showing that the number of schemes had mushroomed by over 500% during the previous decade. In 1994, there were 157 exercise referral schemes in existence, compared with the latest estimate in 2004 of 816. When it was published, the Chief Executive of the CSP, quoted on the CSP website, said: 'This report highlights the way in which exercise referral schemes are of particular benefit to patients at risk of heart attacks and strokes. They are also helping people successfully tackle obesity, diabetes, mental health problems and low-back pain. Physiotherapists play crucial roles in the prevention and management of these conditions and are ideally placed to help roll out a wider network of schemes.'

Andrée Deane, Executive Chair of the Fitness Industry Association at the time, welcomed the initiative: 'Exercise referral schemes provide great opportunities for fitness professionals to work in partnership with health professionals on schemes that target people who do not normally take exercise. These can make a real contribution to public health.'

As a result of a Health Technology Assessment in 2011, NICE updated its guidance on Exercise Referral Schemes to provide recommendations on good practice for better effectiveness. In 2013, it was reported that physical inactivity costs the government £1.06 billion on account of diseases that could be handled by being active, with the cost to industry in sickness absence being £5.5 billion. Therefore, there has been a lot of emphasis placed on district and county councils to increase exercise referral schemes in their area, where time and resources have been spent on improving the amount of provision available for a primary care worker to utilise when referring patients.

## Stand up for your health

On average reports say that British people sit for 8.9 hours every day. Many sit for much more than that. Public Health England has issued guidance designed at employers to help them mobilise their staff to increase productivity because in turn this will improve the health of the workforce. They highlight certain findings that point to an increase in high blood pressure, obesity and type 2 diabetes among workers who spend most of their day sat down.

They recommend that all workers should get between two and four hours of standing and light walking per day; that people check their movements on a regular basis and seek physiotherapy where necessary; balance sitting and standing work and where necessary, encourage employers to equip the workplace with sit-stand desks and also employers should promote the message of a healthy work/life balance.

The role of the physio becomes especially important as the increase in activity under this scheme will mean that some people experience musculoskeletal problems. Not only will physios be responsible for the treatment of these injuries but also there is an emphasis on the profession to circulate guidance on good practice and exercise techniques in order to minimise the numbers of problem cases.

This is not a new initiative and tends to be highlighted annually, certainly over the past few years. However, current research highlights the developing issue and the links with more serious illnesses, which is once again raising the profile of the need for change.

## Physiotherapists given prescribing powers

In 2013, physiotherapists and podiatrists were given the power to prescribe medication to their NHS patients. It is hoped that this will speed up treatment. Physiotherapists have to complete an obligatory training course in order to gain their prescribing rights. Until now, they have had authority to prescribe medication only when working with the written permission of a GP. This move will now give GPs more time to focus on other patients. The BBC reports that 15 million people in the UK with long-term conditions could benefit from this new arrangement.

Phil Gray, Chief Executive of the CSP, is quoted as saying, 'This is a landmark moment that will lead to patients receiving faster, more effective treatment for their condition. Physiotherapists being able to independently prescribe – for the first time anywhere in the world – will remove bureaucracy, free up time for doctors and save money for the NHS.'

# NHS reform 2015

It is fair to say the NHS is constantly in flux. NHS England is reporting in 2015 that there will be a £30 billion shortfall by 2020; however, it is still adjudged to be the best healthcare system in the world.

In July 2010, Andrew Lansley (then Secretary of State for Health) released the White Paper on health reform, 'Equity and Excellence: Liberating the NHS', for implementation in 2011 (for more on this White Paper go to www.bma.org.uk).

The main point of the reform was to return power to patients and their carers and put them in charge of making decisions about their health and well-being. As a result, 2011 was a defining year for the NHS. The health service faced the biggest shake-up since its foundation. Andrew Lansley believed that this would be achieved by devolving an £80 billion budget to around 500 GP consortia, which in turn would buy services, such as operations or scans, from hospitals and other specialists.

The GP consortia would be able to choose whom to buy the services from, possibly even from outside the UK. The 151 primary healthcare trusts would be phased out. The aim was to save the NHS £5 billion (not forgetting that the scheme would cost £1.4 billion to set up) and the changes were to be fully implemented by 2013.

In 2012, the Health and Social Care Act created a new, independent NHS Board whose responsibility was to implement reforms in the NHS in England. In order to cut NHS administration costs, Primary Care Trusts were abolished and new health and well-being boards were set up. Clinical Commissioning Groups took over from the Primary Care Trusts and gave power to GPs in terms of commissioning on behalf of their patients. 'Monitor' was also set up as a sector regulator for health services within the NHS in order to oversee competition within services, with managers of successful hospitals and trusts sent into 14 trusts deemed to be failing in order to improve provision. The changes came into effect on 1 April 2013.

In 2015, the continuing shake-up of the NHS, has meant that under new plans, working hours for doctors and consultants are set to get longer and include weekends, a move that has sparked protest throughout the NHS services this year. Perhaps more controversially, in a move to increase self-assessment for better provision, there is also guidance being brought in advising doctors and practices to signpost patients to the ratings of their hospital and to review themselves. A sign of the changing times as patients can now review services in advance. It will be interesting to see what impact this will have on healthcare services, as there is certainly a lot of opinion for both sides of the argument currently.

## Impact on physiotherapy

The danger is that physiotherapists will be attracted to the private sector, where there is less politics than within the NHS. After a decade of yearly budget rises under the last Labour government, the NHS is to reduce its services through a £20 billion 'efficiency savings' drive. This reduction is most notable in services in England. Cuts to services were announced in 2011, amid claims by the previous government that front-line care would be protected. The cuts meant that those with chronic illnesses saw their NHS physiotherapy services reduced. Specifically, priority 2 and 3 cases either had sessions removed altogether or had their sessions cut by two-thirds. In some cases, those in need of physiotherapy face waits of up to six months, which is sometimes too long.

Since 2011, physiotherapy treatment has been removed for conditions such as back problems or arthritis in the knee; the focus is now on briefly educating patients on their treatment and giving advice on stretching. The CSP revealed that out of 1,000 members surveyed, 74% had seen a rationing of quality services. Some 87% were concerned about the impact this was having on the number of sessions a patient would receive; 81% were concerned about long waiting times; and 71% thought that some people's conditions could become chronic as a result of delays and denial of treatment, in some cases resulting in re-admittance to hospital. Also of concern are those 250,000 people in Britain with severe asthma who face average waiting times of up to six months. This affects not only direct patient care but also the training of parents in how to help their children, particularly those suffering from breathing difficulties. The cuts allowed no time for this training.

CSP members are worried that patient care will suffer under these reforms. CSP Chief Executive Phil Gray said: 'Physiotherapists are concerned that this reorganisation, which is unprecedented in size and scale, will have devastating consequences for patients.' He also went on to say that the budget cuts meant that: 'Patients are facing longer waiting times, fewer sessions with a physiotherapist and, in the most extreme cases, could get no treatment whatsoever.'

Phil Gray told the *Observer*: 'In order to save money, some patients will only receive advice ... That is quite simply a scandal.'

His words were backed up by charities such as Asthma UK, the Multiple Sclerosis Society and the Cystic Fibrosis Trust, which said that patients now have to go to hospital to be allowed access to physiotherapy services that previously were freely available to everyone. The Department of Health has said: 'Efficiency savings should not affect important patient services, at a time when the budget is increasing by a total of £11.5 billion over the next four years.'

The CSP was concerned that the government's revised NHS reforms would increase open market competition in the health service. Therefore it requested that anything that could be deemed to promote competition should be completely removed from the reform proposals, in order to ensure fairness. It submitted an official response to a scrutiny committee of MPs following a review by the independent NHS Future Forum. It said that the Health and Social Care Bill would mean an 'open market' for healthcare providers, which could harm patient services. That said, the CSP welcomed the government's decision to widen the range of clinicians involved in the commissioning process. However, it is still the case that there are no compulsory positions on these new commissioning bodies for allied health professionals such as physiotherapists.

In 2012, the CSP was urging the Coalition government to scrap the reforms, stating that the views of patients and professionals had been ignored. On 25 April 2013, an effort to overturn the Coalition government's decision to implement health service cuts was defeated in the House of Lords. This prompted Phil Gray to say: 'The government's claim that effective services will be protected from competition is undermined by recent history. We have already seen excellent services opened up to the market for no good reason with the expansion of any qualified provider for community health services such as physiotherapy. This has led to restrictions on treatment for patients and confusion for commissioners. These new regulations seem certain to do the same for all other NHS services in an open market.'

A survey by the CSP in 2013 revealed that 60% of physiotherapists in the NHS believed that restricting treatment for financial purposes was having a negative impact on patient care, as it was having an adverse effect on their professional standards. In addition, 29% stated that their trusts were cutting essential services, prompting fears that many patients could miss out on the care they require.

What the CSP would like to see is:

- more services to deal with the treatment of longer term conditions
- self-referral without the need for referral via a GP
- faster access to Occupational Health services
- a greater focus on prevention programmes.

Once again, Phil Gray said: 'This survey paints a worrying picture of how many trusts are not planning ahead for the challenge of funding healthcare in the future. Simply cutting services means conditions that could have been treated quickly and effectively become chronic, long-term problems that will require more expensive treatment or care. Commissioners are under enormous pressure but they must look at the bigger picture to protect patient care. Greater investment in community services will keep people healthy, out of hospital and living indepen-dently at home.'

The main focus of the new NHS reform for physiotherapy is manifold:

- to raise the profile of physiotherapy as a profession
- to work closely with Local Authorities and Public Health
- to develop local education and training boards
- to work within CCGs and sit on Clinical Senates, Health and Wellbeing boards and within Healthwatch
- to develop national outcomes.

The reason for this continual change is to develop service provision tailored to the needs of the local area and, in increasing tendering for services, it is improving the quality of the services on offer based on the competition. As decisions are now based on outcomes, there may be cuts to services within physiotherapy but there may also be positive changes. Therefore, the CSP is understandably encouraging all its members to make their voices heard and fight the need for service provision to be included in these outcome-based services.

## Workout at Work Day

In 2011, as a result of a survey by the CSP that found that four in 10 people get out of breath walking up stairs or running for a bus, the CSP launched Workout at Work Day, with physiotherapists running events to get employees up and moving. The aim was to demonstrate the need for healthier habits and to build more activity into people's daily working lives. The day was organised for 8 September, to coincide with World Physical Therapy Day.

Physiotherapists held events in around 150 workplaces, from John Lewis stores, offices and hospitals to a power station. Employees were offered Pilates classes, lunchtime walking clubs, cycling challenges and table tennis, as well as advice and information sessions. The events gave physiotherapists the opportunity to show what they can offer in terms of occupational health, and also to demonstrate the benefits of daily exercise in everyday life.

Workout at Work Day is now an annual event, with hundreds of events and CSP members taking an active part in the day. The scheme has benefits for employers, as it helps to reduce sick leave and work-place accidents, while promoting proper breaks, in line with contractual law.

# Alternative therapies

Physiotherapists are now becoming increasingly interested in utilising so-called 'alternative therapies' alongside traditional techniques. These can include:

- acupuncture
- Alexander technique
- aromatherapy
- chiropractic medicine
- massage
- reflex therapy.

## Acupuncture

Acupuncture originated over 3,000 years ago in China. The practitioner inserts thin needles into the body at designated places in order to help alleviate or cure problems. Nowadays, this may also involve the use of small electric currents. It is thought that the needles stimulate the body's nervous system into producing its own painkilling substances. The safe delivery of acupuncture is monitored by the Acupuncture Association of Chartered Physiotherapists (AACP), a clinical interest group of the CSP.

## Alexander technique

The Alexander technique is a method of releasing unwanted muscular tension throughout the body by making the patient aware of balance, posture and coordination while performing everyday actions. It is particularly associated with the performing arts.

## Aromatherapy

Aromatherapy uses essential oils that are derived from plants and flowers. The oils are either vaporised and inhaled, or applied directly to the body – often in conjunction with massage.

## Chiropractic medicine

Chiropractic medicine aims to address the improper alignment of the vertebrae in the spine, which, it is believed, causes a number of physical disorders. Re-alignment is achieved by manipulation.

## Massage

Massage is the manipulation of the soft parts of the body. Physiotherapists with a particular interest can do postgraduate training in many different types of massage. The CSP has a special interest group: Chartered Physiotherapists Interested in Massage and Soft Tissue Therapies (CPMaSTT).

## Reflex therapy

Reflex therapy deals with problems within the body by targeting related points on, for example, the feet, hands or head. Reflex therapy can be arranged by consulting a chartered physiotherapist who is a member of the Association of Chartered Physiotherapists in Reflex Therapy (ACPIRT), a clinical interest group of the CSP.

# 8 | Massaging the results
## Results day

The A level results will arrive at your school on the third Thursday in August. The universities will have received them a few days earlier. You must make sure that you go into school on the day the results are published. Do not wait for the results slip to be posted to you. Get your teachers to tell you the news as soon as possible – once they are able to, of course! If you need to act to secure a place you may have to do so quickly. The following paragraphs take you through the steps necessary to use the UCAS Extra, Clearing and Adjustment systems. They also explain what to do if your grades are disappointing.

The university admissions departments are well organised and efficient, but they are staffed by human beings. If there were extenuating circumstances that could have affected your exam performance and which were brought to their notice in June, it is a good idea to ask them to review the relevant letters shortly before the exam results are published.

If you previously received a conditional offer and your grades equal or exceed that offer, congratulations! You can relax and wait for your chosen university to send you joining instructions.

The new UCAS Tariff, which was discussed earlier in the book, will come into play for 2017 entry. Until then, the current Tariff system will be used for entry to courses in September 2016, as well as deferred applications to start in September 2017. Whichever Tariff points are relevant to your application, they could prove important in getting you a place (this is more likely when you have your exam results than at other times of the application cycle where grades remain more important). You may be able to use other qualifications that you hold, such as an AS, to bolster the overall Tariff score; but check with the university that they don't exclude any qualifications such as general studies. Please refer to the UCAS Tariff conversion chart in Chapter 4.

> One word of warning: you cannot assume that grades of AAC satisfy an ABB offer. This is especially true if the C grade is in biology. Always check with your chosen university.

## What to do if you have no offer

If all of the universities that you applied to reject you, you are then eligible to enter a scheme called UCAS Extra. This allows you to apply to other universities, either for physiotherapy or for other courses. You will automatically be sent details by UCAS.

UCAS Extra starts in March. If UCAS Extra does not provide you with an offer, you can enter Clearing in August. These days, very few applicants get into university through Clearing. Very few universities have spare places in August and, of those that do, most will choose to allow applicants who hold a conditional offer to slip a grade rather than dust off a reserve list of those they interviewed but did not make an offer to. Still less are they likely to consider applicants who appear out of the blue, however high their grades. That said, it is likely that every summer one or two universities will have enough unfilled places to consider a Clearing-style application.

If you hold, say, AAB but were rejected when you applied through UCAS, you need to let the universities know that you are out there. The best way to do this is by email. If you live nearby you can always deliver a letter in person, talk to the office staff and hope that your application will stand out from the rest.

Below you will find a sample email. Do not copy it word for word! Do not forget that your UCAS referee may be able to help you. Try to persuade him or her to ring the admissions officers on your behalf – your referee

From: Jo Carter
To: mdwhyte@grantchester.ac.uk
Subject: Physiotherapy places

Dear Miss Whyte
UCAS No. 15-123456-8

I have just received my A level results, which were: Biology A, Chemistry C, English C. I also have an A grade in AS English Language. You may remember that I applied to Grantchester but was rejected after interview/was rejected without an interview. I am still very keen to study physiotherapy at Grantchester and hope that you will consider me for any places that may now be available. My head teacher supports my application and is faxing you a reference. Should you wish to contact him, the details are: Mr S. Honry, tel: 0123 456 7891, fax: 0123 456 7892. I can be contacted at the above email address and could attend an interview at short notice.

Jo Carter

will find it easier to get through than you will. If your head teacher is unable or unwilling to ring, then he or she should at least email a note in support of your application. It is best if both emails arrive at the university at the same time.

If you are applying to a university that did not receive your UCAS application, ask your head to email or send a copy of the application. In general it is best to persuade the university to invite you to arrange for the UCAS application to be sent.

If, despite your most strenuous efforts, you are unsuccessful, you need to consider applying again (see page 93). The alternative is to use the Clearing system to obtain a place on a degree course related to physiotherapy and to hope to be accepted on a physiotherapy course after you graduate. This option is described on page 90.

## What to do if you hold an offer but miss the grades

If you have only narrowly missed the required grades (this includes the AAC grade case described above) it is important that you and your referee email the university to put your case before you are rejected. Another sample email follows below.

From: Jo Carter
To: mdwhyte@grantchester.ac.uk
Subject: A level results

Dear Miss Whyte
UCAS No. 15-123456-8

I have just received my A level results, which were: Biology A, Chemistry B, English C. I hold a conditional offer from Grantchester of ABB and I realise that my grades fall below that offer. Nevertheless, I am still determined to study physiotherapy and I hope you will be able to find a place for me this year. I would like to remind you that at the time of the exams I was recovering from glandular fever. A medical certificate was sent to you in June by my head teacher.

My head teacher supports my application and is faxing you a reference. Should you wish to contact him, the details are: Mr S. Honry, tel: 0123 456 7891, fax: 0123 456 7892. I can be contacted at the above email address and could attend an interview at short notice.

Jo Carter

## What if your grades are significantly better than anticipated?

UCAS now operates a scheme called Adjustment, which is aimed at applicants who have achieved grades better than predicted. It is primarily designed for students who might have been predicted low grades and who, therefore, applied for places at universities that would accept them, rather than where they really wanted to go. The Adjustment system allows these students to hold on to their offers for a short period while contacting other universities where the standard offers are higher to see whether they can be considered. Full details can be found on the UCAS website.

## Retaking your A levels

Universities' grade requirements for retake candidates are often higher than for first-timers. You should contact the universities to find out what they require from retake students. Many A levels can be retaken, but a student can re-sit only in June, which poses problems of its own. As you will note from the A level reforms section (see Chapter 4), these A levels can only be re-sat for a finite period longer. The timescale for your retakes will depend on:

- the grades you obtained first time
- the examination board through which you studied.

If you simply need to improve one subject by one or two grades and can retake the exam on the same syllabus, then a short retake course between January and June is the logical option. However, you do need to consider whether it is realistic for you to re-start study, having not studied the subject for seven months. You also need to consider whether spending a full year on your retakes would give universities more confidence that you will achieve the required grades. The school or college where you will sit the retakes will be able to advise you.

If, on the other hand, your grades were DDE you probably need to spend another year on your retakes.

Independent sixth-form colleges provide specialist advice and teaching for students considering A level retakes. Interviews to discuss this are free and carry no obligation to enrol on a course, so it is worth taking the time to talk to their staff before you embark on A level retakes.

The most important thing to be aware of is that if you are retaking your A levels, your opportunities to do so are finite under the government's new educational reform that came into effect in September 2015. The last re-take of all AS and A2 modules in Phase one subjects (see Chapter 4) will be in June 2017, after which point you will not be able to retake A levels.

It is worthwhile bearing in mind that students who are now retaking are not only going to be compared with first-time applicants but also first-time applicants from a new academic system and that may have an effect on decisions.

## Re-applying to university

The choice of universities for your UCAS application will be narrower than it was the first time round. Do not apply to universities that discourage retakers unless there really are special, extenuating circumstances to explain your disappointing grades. The following are examples of excuses that would not be regarded by admissions tutors as extenuating circumstances.

- 'I was revising on my dad's yacht and my files got soaked when I accidentally dropped them in the sea.'
- 'I left my bag on the bus the week before the exams, and all of my notes were in it, so I couldn't do any revision.'
- 'We moved house a month before the exams and a removal man trod on my notes, so I couldn't revise properly from them.'

Some reasons are acceptable to even the most fanatical opponents of retake candidates:

- your own illness
- the death or serious illness of a very close relative.

*Please note, an extenuating circumstance application is not a different application. The circumstances are really the responsibility of your referee to explain.*

These are just guidelines, and the only sure way to find out if a university will accept you is to write and ask. A typical email is set out at the end of this chapter. Do not follow it word for word and do take the time to write to several universities before you make your final choice.

Notice that the format of your email should be:

- opening paragraph
- your exam results: set out clearly, with no omissions
- any extenuating circumstances: a brief statement
- your retake plan: including the timescale
- a request for help and advice
- closing paragraph.

Make sure that your email is brief, clear and well presented. Even if you go to this trouble, the pressure on universities in the autumn is such that you may receive no more than a standard reply to the effect that, if you apply, your application will be considered. Apart from the care needed in making your choice of universities, the rest of the application procedure is as described in the first part of this book.

From: Jo Carter
To: mdwhyte@grantchester.ac.uk
Subject: Application for physiotherapy

Dear Miss Whyte
Last year's UCAS No. 15-123456-8

I am writing to ask your advice because I am about to complete my UCAS application and would very much like to apply to Grantchester. You may remember that I applied to you last year and received an offer of ABB/was rejected after interview/was rejected without an interview. I have just received my A level results, which were: Biology B, Chemistry C, History D. I was aged 16 years and seven months at the time of taking these exams.

I plan to retake Chemistry in June after a 17-week course in the period from January to June, and History over a year. If necessary, I will also retake Biology in June. I am confident that I can push these subjects up to ABB grades overall.

What worries me is that I have heard that some universities do not consider retake candidates even when the exams were taken under the age of 18 and relatively high grades were obtained. I am very keen not to waste anyone's time by applying to departments that will reject me purely because I am retaking.

I am very keen to study at Grantchester, and would be extremely grateful for any advice that you can give me.

Jo Carter

# 9 | The fifth metatarsal
## Non-standard applications

So far, this book has been concerned with the 'standard' applicant: the UK resident who is studying at least two science subjects at A level and who is applying from school or who is retaking immediately after disappointing A levels. This chapter outlines the application process for 'non-standard' applicants.

The main non-standard categories are as follows.

## Students who have not studied science A levels

If you decide that you would like to study physiotherapy after having already started on a combination of A levels that does not fit the subject requirements for entry to university, you have three choices.

1. You can spend an extra year studying science A levels at a sixth-form college that offers one-year AS/A2 courses. These still exist under the new A level reforms and will continue on the old specifications until the deadlines for retakes have passed, being in 2017 with the end of Phase One subjects. There will be reformed one-year courses from that point going forwards. You should discuss your particular circumstances with prospective colleges in order to select suitable courses. You need to be aware that only very able students can cover A level Chemistry and Biology in a single year with good results.
2. You can follow a Foundation course at a university that will then allow you to study a related degree course afterwards. For details of Foundation courses you should contact universities.
3. You can enrol on an Access course which is recognised by the universities you wish to apply to. Each university will have different policies about Access courses – you should contact the physiotherapy departments directly.

## International students

The competition for the few places available to non-EU students is fierce and you would be wise to discuss your application informally with the university before submitting it. In general, overseas applicants will find it difficult to gain a place unless they can offer qualifications that are recognised by the universities, such as A levels or the International Baccalaureate (IB).

Information about qualifications can be obtained from British Council offices, British embassies and the universities that offer physiotherapy courses. Overseas students are liable for the full cost of tuition. For physiotherapy the fees vary depending on the university, but will be in the region of £13,000–£17,500 per year. The UCAS website has a section for international students that describes in detail the application process and deadlines.

### English language qualifications

In order to begin a university degree in this country, you are required to have an accredited English language qualification if you are a European or international student. This is because it is essential that you are able to understand the course and what is being taught to you throughout your studies.

You should aim to achieve at least IELTS (International English Language Testing System) 6.5 to 7.0 in order to begin a university course, and certainly no less than 6.5 in each band. Most universities will set the boundary higher, commonly at 7.0 now, in order to discourage some applications. If you would like further information on IELTS, please visit www.ielts.org.

TOEFL (Test of English as a Foreign Language) is also acceptable and you should aim for a score in excess of 100 out of 120. If you would like further information on TOEFL, please visit www.ets.org/toefl.

### Visa requirements

If you require a visa to be in the UK and your course is longer than six months, which physiotherapy courses invariably are, then you will need to apply for a Tier 4 Student Visa. In order to do this, the university you are accepted by will request from you various pieces of information, including your education transcripts and passport. They will produce a Confirmation of Acceptance of Studies (CAS) letter for you once you have given them all the information and paid a nominated deposit; you will take the CAS letter to the UK embassy in your country in order to obtain a visa for studying. Do not delay in this process as obtaining a visa can take time, which varies from country to country.

# Mature students

Physiotherapy courses are popular with older students, and the universities tend to have a flexible and encouraging approach to students over the age of 21.

Approximately 30% of students studying physiotherapy are mature students. Work experience is key, as it points to you being a strong candidate and having researched the course properly.

# Graduates

A 2.i degree (or higher) along with at least a grade B in A level Biology is normally required for graduates applying for physiotherapy. Most universities ask graduates to take a year out between the final year of their first degree course and the start of the physiotherapy course in order to get work experience. This allows them to demonstrate that they are serious about a career in physiotherapy.

# Applicants with no suitable academic qualifications

Candidates are likely to be asked to sit at least two A levels, one of which will be biology, and to achieve B grades or higher. There are also some Access courses that can lead to an offer of a place to study physiotherapy; applicants should liaise with universities to confirm suitability.

The main difficulty facing those coming late to the idea of studying physiotherapy is that they rarely have a scientific background. They face the daunting task of studying science A levels and need very careful counselling before they embark on what will, inevitably, be quite a tough programme. Independent sixth-form colleges provide this counselling as part of their normal interview procedure.

# Students not studying A levels

As with A levels, entrance requirements will vary from university to university. The information below is given as a guideline only.

- BTEC Higher National Diploma: 16 units, mostly biology or life sciences, with merits and distinctions throughout.
- BTEC National Certificate: 18 units, mostly biology and life sciences, with merits and distinctions throughout; plus one A level or two AS qualifications. The rules are tightening up the requirements relating to the BTEC and it is now common for you to need to achieve a distinction and have at least A level Biology as well.
- Cambridge Pre-U: combinations of three subjects allowed, usually looking towards a D3/M1 or higher.
- Advanced Vocational Certificate of Education: 12 units with science or healthcare-related options, possibly with one A level or two AS qualifications.

- Irish Leaving Certificate: six papers taken at one sitting, at Higher level, to include at least AABBB, or 162 points (under the new Tariff, or 400+ for 2016 entry).
- Scottish Highers: 132 points (under the new Tariff, or 320 for 2016 entry), to include two sciences.
- IB: 32+ points, with biology at Higher level.

Other qualifications, such as the European Baccalaureate, the French Baccalaureate or Open University qualifications, or the successful completion of a recognised Access course, will usually be considered, but there is no guarantee that an offer will be made.

## Access courses

A proportion of colleges of further education offer Access courses suitable for physiotherapy. The best known and most successful of these, though not the only one, is the course at the College of West Anglia in King's Lynn. Primarily (but not exclusively) aimed at health professionals, the Access to Science and Nursing course lasts one year and covers:

- human biology
- forensic science
- health and community studies
- physics
- chemistry
- psychology
- geography
- level 3 mathematics.

It should be noted there are also other providers.

The course that you take might be Access to Science, to Health Studies, to Physiotherapy or to Medical Sciences, but you must cover cardiovascular, pulmonary and skeletal muscle physiology at level 3. Some universities will ask for biology or human biology. You should contact the specific university to find out exactly which Access course it recognises.

You should contact the university admissions tutors or look on the university websites for advice. There is a strong case for suggesting that those people getting in to universities are the ones who put in the work beforehand by talking to the universities. If you have a question, ask it – you will get an answer that you can then base your decision on.

# 10 | Make no bones about it
## Fees and funding

The following sections explain what the governmental changes mean in respect of university tuition fees and give you some ideas of where you may find help in funding your studies.

## Fees

### UK students

A big argument at the moment is being put forward by universities who believe that the current funding arrangements for staffing and students 'are unsustainable'. The government is cutting back on public spending and pre-registration education is responsible for £1 billion costs per year. What universities want is a funding review at a time when the NHS is putting in place a five-year education plan.

At present, the NHS student and education funding in England is £1.4 billion, with Health Education England paying the 'benchmark price' for each student place.

As a result of governmental changes, universities are allowed to charge UK and EU students up to £9,000 a year for tuition fees. In fact, the Chancellor said in the July 2015 budget that for those institutions offering high quality education, they would be allowed to charge above inflation on the £9,000 from 2017/18, a move met with concern by the CSP as they think it will discourage students from less privileged backgrounds from the profession. This potential rise sparked student protests, with student demonstrations staged in London. Almost all of the higher-ranked universities will charge the maximum amount. The average course fee across all institutions is £9,000 in 2015. According to the *Complete University Guide*, 113 out of 120 universities in England and Wales are charging the full tuition fee. If you are a student resident in England you will pay up to £9,000, wherever you study in the UK. If you are a student resident in Scotland you will pay a set £1,820 tuition fee if you study at a Scottish university, with the Students Awards Agency for Scotland paying those fees if you meet eligibility criteria; you will pay up to £9,000 if you study elsewhere in the UK. If you are a student resident in Wales you will pay up to £9,000 wherever you study in the UK; however, you will be able to receive a £3,810 loan from the Welsh Government, and you will also be eligible for a grant up to the difference between the loan and the full fee. If you are a student resident in Northern Ireland you will pay up to £9,000 if you study in England, Wales or Scotland, but you will pay only £3,805 if you study in Northern Ireland. You should refer to the websites of the specific universities to find out what they intend to charge, and also to the UCAS website, using the course search facility.

## EU students

If you are an EU student you will pay up to £9,000 if you study in England or £3,805 in Northern Ireland, but only £1,820 if you study in Scotland. You will receive the same help as Welsh students (see above) if you are studying at a Welsh university.

## Non-EU international students

The fees for non-EU international students do not have a set upper limit. The fees will depend on the course and the university. For example, Brunel charges £16,500 per year, while Queen's Belfast will charge £17,035 per year.

# Bursaries, sponsorship and grants

## NHS bursaries

Typically, eligible UK students studying physiotherapy will not pay tuition fees, as these are paid by the NHS. These students will also receive a non-means-tested NHS grant, currently £1,000 p.a., and are eligible for a means-tested NHS bursary to help with day-to-day living costs. All new and prospective students are eligible to apply and students who are awarded these bursaries can also apply for student loans.

### NHS bursary applications checklist (according to the NHS Business Services Authority)

- Regardless of nationality, you must be considered to be ordinarily living in the UK and/or the Channel Islands or the Isle of Man, as well as being settled in the UK under the Immigration Act 1971.
- In order to apply for the bursary, you must have received a conditional or unconditional offer from any university or higher education institution in England.

- Once your details have been received, the university or higher education institution will pass them on to NHS Student Bursaries, which will then contact you with your student reference number and information on where you can obtain the relevant application form on its website.
- All students applying for a bursary are required to submit original identity documentation with their forms, i.e. a driver's licence or a passport.
- Applications should be submitted as soon as possible. The NHS bursary application form should be submitted not less than six months prior to the first day of the course. For example, if your first day is 1 September 2017, then the last date when you can submit the application form is 1 March 2017.

For an indication of how much you might be eligible for, please refer to Table 5, which is published by the NHS Business Services Authority.

Home students and EU citizens who are not in receipt of an NHS bursary are required to be self-funding. This is the case for any UK or EU citizens who do not normally live in the UK who need to pay the annual rate of £9,000 p.a.

| If you are studying: | You may receive up to: |
|---|---|
| At a university located **in London** and you will be living in student/rented accommodation or your own home | £3,571 (max) |
| At a university located **elsewhere in the UK** and you will be living in student/rented accommodation or your own home | £2,958 (max) |
| At a university located anywhere in the UK (including London) and you will be **living with your parent or parents in their home** | £2,470 (max) |

**Table 5:** Guideline student bursary eligibility (basic bursary rates 2015–16)

## Contact details for awarding bodies

### England
NHS Student Grants Unit
Email: enquiries@nhspa.gov.uk
Website: www.nhsbsa.nhs.uk/Students.aspx

### Wales
NHS Wales Student Awards Services
Email: abm.sas@wales.nhs.uk
Website: www.nwsspstudentfinance.wales.nhs.uk/home

**Scotland**
Student Awards Agency Scotland
Website: www.saas.gov.uk

**Northern Ireland**
Department for Employment and Learning
Website: www.studentfinanceni.co.uk

### Sponsorship

Sponsorship is also sometimes available from prospective future employers; the Armed Forces are particularly well known to support students through their training. If you wish to apply for sponsorship from a specific sports club or national body – and bear in mind that some of them will not advertise such schemes – then it is often best to get in touch personally in writing, stating your aims and career aspirations and the course onto which you have been accepted to study.

### Maintenance loans

You will still need to find money to pay for your rent, bills, books, food, drink and any hobbies or interests. In England, there used to be maintenance grants available for students from lower-income households. However, the Chancellor abolished these in the July 2015 budget, declaring them 'unaffordable', and they will cease to be offered for courses starting in September 2016 or later. Instead, all money available to students for living expenses will be provided as a maintenance loan, to be paid back once students start earning £21,000 or more. Figures for students from different parts of the UK will vary slightly. For further details please refer to the UCAS website, www.ucas.com.

Universities charging tuition fees of £9,000 must provide financial support for students from disadvantaged backgrounds. You can find out about this at:

- www.ucas.com/ucas/undergraduate/finance-and-support
- www.direct.gov.uk/en/EducationAndLearning/UniversityAndHigher Education/StudentFinance/index.htm.

## Work while you study

The first people to check with about working while you study are the universities themselves, as some have a policy that you cannot pursue any paid employment while studying this course; but most will merely point out the time commitment involved in the work experience you will be doing as part of your course. That is certainly something to bear in mind as it will be draining in both time and energy for you.

Of course, it is understandable that you may need to find part-time work alongside your course in order to supplement your living and mainte-nance costs, but just make sure that it does not become a primary emphasis. This is not a course that can be approached half-heartedly and you must make sure that the majority of your spare time is spent pursuing the ultimate end goal.

# 11| Exercise the mind
## Useful information and further resources

You are advised to check the UCAS Handbook or website for information on courses and universities before applying.

## Universities offering physiotherapy degrees

**University of Birmingham**
Tel: 0121 414 8327
Website: www.birmingham.ac.uk

**Bournemouth University**
Tel: 01202 524111
Website: www.bournemouth.ac.uk

**University of Bradford**
Tel: 01274 236367
Website: www.bradford.ac.uk

**University of Brighton**
Tel: 01273 643772
Website: www.brighton.ac.uk

**Bristol, University of the West of England**
Tel: 0117 328 3333
Website: www.uwe.ac.uk

**Brunel University**
Tel: 01895 268683
Website: www.brunel.ac.uk

**Cardiff University**
Tel: 029 2087 4000
Website: www.cardiff.ac.uk

**University of Central Lancashire**
Tel: 01772 892400
Website: www.uclan.ac.uk

**Coventry University**
Tel: 024 7765 5959
Website: www.coventry.ac.uk

**University of Cumbria**
Tel: 01228 616234 (Carlisle)
Website: www.cumbria.ac.uk

**University of East Anglia**
Tel: 01603 456161
Website: www.uea.ac.uk

**University of East London**
Tel: 020 8223 3000
Website: www.uel.ac.uk

**Glasgow Caledonian University**
Tel: 0141 331 8630
Website: www.gcal.ac.uk

**University of Hertfordshire**
Tel: 01707 284800
Website: www.herts.ac.uk

**University of Huddersfield**
Tel: 01484 473566
Website: www.hud.ac.uk

**Keele University**
Tel: 01782 734191
Website: www.keele.ac.uk

**King's College London**
Tel: 020 7836 5454
Website: www.kcl.ac.uk

**Kingston University (St George's University London)**
Tel: 020 8417 9000
Website: www.kingston.ac.uk

**Leeds Beckett University**
Tel: 0113 812 3113
Website: www.leedsbeckett.ac.uk

**University of Liverpool**
Tel: 0151 794 5712
Website: www.liv.ac.uk

**Manchester Metropolitan University**
Tel: 0161 247 6969
Website: www.mmu.ac.uk

**Northumbria University**
Tel: 0191 243 7900
Website: www.northumbria.ac.uk

**University of Nottingham**
Tel: 0115 823 1867
Website: www.nottingham.ac.uk

**Oxford Brookes University**
Tel: 01865 484848
Website: www.brookes.ac.uk

**Plymouth University**
Tel: 01752 585858
Website: www.plymouth.ac.uk

**Queen Margaret University, Edinburgh**
Tel: 0131 474 0000
Website: www.qmu.ac.uk

**Robert Gordon University, Aberdeen**
Tel: 01224 262000
Website: www.rgu.ac.uk

**University of Salford**
Tel: 0161 295 5000
Website: www.salford.ac.uk

**Sheffield Hallam University**
Tel: 0114 225 5555
Website: www.shu.ac.uk

**University of Southampton**
Tel: 023 8059 5000
Website: www.southampton.ac.uk

**St George's, University of London**
Tel: 020 8672 9944
Website: www.sgul.ac.uk

**Teesside University**
Tel: 01642 384110
Website: www.tees.ac.uk

**University of Ulster**
Tel: 028 9036 6220
Website: www.ulster.ac.uk

**University of Worcester**
Tel: 01905 855111
Website: www.worcester.ac.uk

**York St John University**
Tel: 01904 624624
Website: www.yorksj.ac.uk

## New Tariff from 2017 entry onwards

To give you some context, the tables below show a comparison of the old and new UCAS Tariffs and what each grade is worth under each system:

| Grade | Tariff for entry until September 2016 | Tariff from September 2017 entry onwards |
|---|---|---|
| A* | 140 | 56 |
| A | 120 | 48 |
| B | 100 | 40 |
| C | 80 | 32 |
| D | 60 | 24 |
| E | 40 | 16 |

**Table 6:** A level

| Grade | Tariff for entry until September 2016 | Tariff from September 2017 entry onwards |
|---|---|---|
| A | 60 | 20 |
| B | 50 | 16 |
| C | 40 | 12 |
| D | 30 | 10 |
| E | 20 | 6 |

**Table 7:** AS (if required)

At the point of going to press, most universities will not have decided on their entry requirements for 2017 yet, therefore have a look at the table below to see what their equivalencies would be currently. Please refer directly to the UCAS search tool (search.ucas.com) and the universities' websites at the time of application for the most up-to-date information on entrance requirements.

| Grades | Tariff for entry until September 2016 | Tariff from September 2017 entry onwards |
|---|---|---|
| A*AA | 380 | 152 |
| AAA | 360 | 144 |
| AAB | 340 | 136 |
| ABB | 320 | 128 |

**Table 8:** Entry requirements equivalency

There are different variations for other qualifications and I would suggest referring directly to www.ucas.com/sites/default/files/new-tariff-tables.pdf, for more information.

# Useful resources

### Chartered Society of Physiotherapy

An essential starting point is the CSP's website (www.csp.org.uk). It carries detailed information about careers in physiotherapy and recognised courses. The CSP also produces many useful booklets about physiotherapy. It can be contacted at:

Chartered Society of Physiotherapy
14 Bedford Row
London WC1R 4ED
Tel: 020 7306 6666

The CSP publishes a magazine, *Frontline*, aimed at practising physiotherapists. The magazine contains articles of interest and is a useful way of keeping up to date with current issues and new developments. There is also a large jobs section – a good way to make contact with physiotherapy practices if you are looking for work experience.

### Other societies

The Irish Society of Chartered Physiotherapists
Royal College of Surgeons
St Stephen's Green
Dublin 2
D02 H903
Ireland
Tel: +353 1 402 2148
Website: www.iscp.ie

The College of Occupational Therapists
106–14 Borough High Street
London SE1 1LB
Tel: 020 7357 6480
Website: www.cot.co.uk

The College of Podiatry
1 Fellmonger's Path
Tower Bridge Road
London SE1 3LY
Tel: 020 7234 8620
Website: www.scpod.org

# UCAS

For information on university applications contact UCAS (www.ucas.com). The UCAS website has a search facility that will enable you to check the latest entrance requirements for all universities that offer physiotherapy courses. Application materials can be obtained from:

UCAS
Rosehill
New Barn Lane
Cheltenham GL52 3LZ

## Other useful addresses

Department for Employment and Learning (Northern Ireland)
Adelaide House
39–49 Adelaide Street
Belfast BT2 8FD
Tel: 028 9025 7777
Website: www.delni.gov.uk

NHS (England) Student Bursaries
PO Box 141
Hesketh House
200–220 Broadway
Fleetwood FY7 8SS
Tel: 0300 330 1342
Website: www.nhsbsa.nhs.uk

For visually-impaired applicants:
RNIB Physiotherapy Resource Centre
University of East London
Romford Road
London E15 4LZ
Tel: 020 8223 4950

Students Awards Agency Scotland
Saughton House
Broomhouse Drive
Edinburgh EH11 3UT
Website: www.saas.gov.uk

Student Awards Services (NHS Wales)
Floor 4
Companies House
Crown Way
Cardiff CF14 3UB
Tel: 029 2090 5380
Website: www.nwsspstudentfinance.wales.nhs.uk/home

# Useful websites

## Examination boards

www.aqa.org.uk
www.ets.org/toefl
www.ielts.org
www.ocr.org.uk
http://qualifications.pearson.com
www.wjec.co.uk

## Online physiotherapy information

www.evidence.nhs.uk
www.lifemark.ca
www.akeso.co
www.naidex.co.uk
www.thephysiotherapysite.co.uk

## University league tables

www.theguardian.com/education/universityguide

## Work experience

www.prospects.co.uk

## Fees and funding

www.studentfinanceni.co.uk
www.studentfinancewales.co.uk
www.ucas.com/ucas/undergraduate/finance-and-support
www.gov.uk/student-finance

# Further reading

## Books on careers/university applications

*How to Complete Your UCAS Application*, Beryl Dixon, MPW Guides/ Trotman Education

*University Degree Course Offers: The essential guide to winning your place at university*, Brian Heap, Trotman Education

## Books on physiotherapy

There are numerous textbooks covering all aspects of physiotherapy. Most of these are aimed at undergraduates or physiotherapy professionals. The following will give A level (or the equivalent) students an overview of what studying physiotherapy would entail:

*A Practical Guide to Sports Injuries*, Malcolm T. F. Read, Butterworth-Heinemann

*Principles and Practice of Physical Therapy*, William E. Arnould-Taylor, Stanley Thornes

# 12| Don't be bone idle
## Glossary

| | |
|---|---|
| CCG | clinical commissioning group |
| CfWI | Centre for Workforce Intelligence |
| CPD | continuing professional development |
| CSP | The Chartered Society of Physiotherapy |
| CTD | cumulative trauma disorder |
| ESWT | extracorporeal shockwave therapy |
| *Frontline* | CSP magazine |
| Gait re-education | learning to walk with a normal pattern again |
| HCPC | Health & Care Professions Council |
| HESA | Higher Education Statistics Agency |
| HPAT | Health Professions Admission Test (Ireland) |
| Hydrotherapy | using water in treating pain relief and illness |
| Infrared and ultraviolet radiation | used to warm damaged muscles and speed up healing |
| IPE | inter-professional education |
| MCSP | Member of the Chartered Society of Physiotherapists |
| MDT | multidisciplinary team |
| NHS | National Health Service |
| OOS | occupational overuse syndrome |
| PBL | problem-based learning |
| PBPL | practice-based professional learning |
| Personal statement | part of the UCAS application (4,000 characters with spaces), aimed at persuading universities to accept your application |
| RSI | repetitive strain injury |
| SRP | State Registered Physiotherapist |
| Tennis elbow | calcification of a tendon |
| UCAS | The Universities and Colleges Admissions Service |

| Ultrasound | using sound waves to break down scar tissue and reduce inflammation |
| WRMSD | work-related musculoskeletal disorder |
| WRULD | work-related upper limb disorder |

# Postscript

If you have any comments or questions arising out of this book, we and the staff of MPW would be very happy to answer them. You can contact us at the addresses below.

Good luck with your applications!
James Barton

MPW (London)
90–92 Queen's Gate
London SW7 5AB
Tel: 020 7835 1355
Fax: 020 7259 2705
Email: london@mpw.co.uk

MPW (Cambridge)
3–4 Brookside
Cambridge CB2 1JE
Tel: 01223 350158
Fax: 01223 366429
Email: cambridge@mpw.co.uk

MPW (Birmingham)
17–18 Greenfield Crescent
Edgbaston
Birmingham B15 3AU
Tel: 0121 454 9637
Fax: 0121 454 6433
Email: birmingham@mpw.co.uk

# Titles in the
# Getting into series

**Getting into**
Medical School
2017 Entry

James Barton and Simon Horner

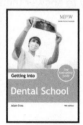

**Getting into**
Dental School

Adam Cross

**Getting into**
Veterinary
School

James Barton

How to
Complete Your
UCAS Application
2017 Entry

Beryl Dixon

**Getting into**
Psychology
Courses

John Cowter

**Getting into**
Physiotherapy
Courses

James Barton

**Getting into**
Pharmacy and
Pharmacology
Courses

Bridget Hutchings

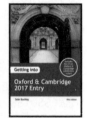

**Getting into**
Oxford & Cambridge
2017 Entry

Seân Buckley

**Getting into**
Art & Design
Courses

James Burnett

**Getting into**
Law

Simon Royes and Melanie Allen

**Getting into**
Business &
Economics Courses

Carly Roberts

**Getting into**
Engineering
Courses

James Burnett

Written by experts in a clear and concise format,
these guides go beyond the official publications to
give would-be students practical advice on how to
secure a place on the course of their choice.

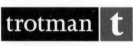

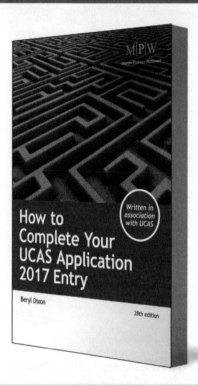

# The essential guide to winning your place at university

**'The guru of university choice.'**
*The Times*

The only independent guide that gives you all the information you need to find the course and university of your choice.

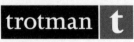